THE ENCYCLOPEDIA OF PSYCHOACTIVE DRUGS

SERIES 1

SERIES 2

CELEBRITY DRUG USE

SOLOMON H. SNYDER, M.D. • GENERAL EDITOR

THE ENCYCLOPEDIA OF PSYCHOACTIVE DRUGS

SERIES 2

CELEBRITY DRUG USE

MARC KUSINITZ

CHELSEA HOUSE PUBLISHERS

NEW YORK • PHILADELPHIA

EDITOR-IN-CHIEF: Nancy Toff
EXECUTIVE EDITOR: Remmel T. Nunn
MANAGING EDITOR: Karyn Gullen Browne
COPY CHIEF: Juliann Barbato
PICTURE EDITOR: Adrian Allen
ART DIRECTOR: Giannella Garrett
MANUFACTURING MANAGER: Gerald Levine

Staff for CELEBRITY DRUG USE:

SENIOR EDITOR: Jane Larkin Crain
ASSOCIATE EDITOR: Paula Edelson
ASSISTANT EDITOR: Michele A. Merens
EDITORIAL ASSISTANT: Laura-Ann Dolce
CAPTIONS: Louise Bloomfield
COPY EDITORS: Sean Dolan, Gillian Bucky, Ellen Scordato, Michael Goodman
ASSOCIATE PICTURE EDITOR: Juliette Dickstein
PICTURE RESEARCHER: Susan Hamburger
DESIGNER: Victoria Tomaselli
PRODUCTION COORDINATOR: Laura McCormick
COVER ILLUSTRATION: Jane Sterrett

CREATIVE DIRECTOR: Harold Steinberg

5   7   9   8   6   4

Library of Congress Cataloging in Publication Data

Kusinitz, Marc.
   Celebrity drug use.
   (The Encyclopedia of psychoactive drugs. Series 2)
   Bibliography: p.
   Includes index.
   1. Celebrities—Drug use—Juvenile literature.
2. Celebrities—Alcohol use—Juvenile literature. 3. Drug
abuse—Juvenile literature. [1. Celebrities—Drug
use.   2. Celebrities—Alcohol use.   3. Drug use]
I. Title. II. Series.
HV5824.C42K87   1987   362.2'92'0922   87–6646

ISBN 1-55546-225-1
   0-7910-0780-4 (pbk.)

CONTENTS

Kirk Cameron, the popular star of the television comedy series "Growing Pains," is an outspoken opponent of drug use. He has focused his efforts on fighting cocaine abuse among teenagers.

In the Mainstream
of American Life

One of the legacies of the social upheaval of the 1960s is that psychoactive drugs have become part of the mainstream of American life. Schools, homes, and communities cannot be "drug proofed." There is a demand for drugs — and the supply is plentiful. Social norms have changed and drugs are not only available—they are everywhere.

But where efforts to curtail the supply of drugs and outlaw their use have had tragically limited effects on demand, it may be that education has begun to stem the rising tide of drug abuse among young people and adults alike.

Over the past 25 years, as drugs have become an increasingly routine facet of contemporary life, a great many teenagers have adopted the notion that drug taking was somehow a right or a privilege or a necessity. They have done so, however, without understanding the consequences of drug use during the crucial years of adolescence.

The teenage years are few in the total life cycle, but critical in the maturation process. During these years adolescents face the difficult tasks of discovering their identity, clarifying their sexual roles, asserting their independence, learning to cope with authority, and searching for goals that will give their lives meaning.

Drugs rob adolescents of precious time, stamina, and health. They interrupt critical learning processes, sometimes forever. Teenagers who use drugs are likely to withdraw increasingly into themselves, to "cop out" at just the time when they most need to reach out and experience the world.

Hollywood, the center of the entertainment industry for decades, has spelled fame and success for some people, but its relentless pressures have driven many stars to drug abuse — with tragic consequences.

Fortunately, as a recent Gallup poll shows, young people are beginning to realize this, too. They themselves label drugs their most important problem. In the last few years, moreover, the climate of tolerance and ignorance surrounding drugs has been changing.

Adolescents as well as adults are becoming aware of mounting evidence that every race, ethnic group, and class is vulnerable to drug dependency.

Recent publicity about the cost and failure of drug rehabilitation efforts; dangerous drug use among pilots, air traffic controllers, star athletes, and Hollywood celebrities; and drug-related accidents, suicides, and violent crime have focused the public's attention on the need to wage an all-out war on drug abuse before it seriously undermines the fabric of society itself.

The anti-drug message is getting stronger and there is evidence that the message is beginning to get through to adults and teenagers alike.

The Encyclopedia of Psychoactive Drugs hopes to play a part in the national campaign now underway to educate young people about drugs. Series 1 provides clear and comprehensive discussions of common psychoactive substances, outlines their psychological and physiological effects on the mind and body, explains how they "hook" the user, and separates fact from myth in the complex issue of drug abuse.

Whereas Series 1 focuses on specific drugs, such as nicotine or cocaine, Series 2 confronts a broad range of both social and physiological phenomena. Each volume addresses the ramifications of drug use and abuse on some aspect of human experience: social, familial, cultural, historical, and physical. Separate volumes explore questions about the effects of drugs on brain chemistry and unborn children; the use and abuse of painkillers; the relationship between drugs and sexual behavior, sports, and the arts; drugs and disease; the role of drugs in history; and the sophisticated drugs now being developed in the laboratory that will profoundly change the future.

Each book in the series is fully illustrated and is tailored to the needs and interests of young readers. The more adolescents know about drugs and their role in society, the less likely they are to misuse them.

Joann Rodgers
Senior Editorial Consultant

Rock stars are often associated with drug abuse, but many successful musicians — such as Tina Turner and Mick Jagger — claim that the electricity of a live performance is more exhilarating than any drug.

INTRODUCTION

The Gift of Wizardry
Use and Abuse

JACK H. MENDELSON, M.D.
NANCY K. MELLO, Ph.D.
Alcohol and Drug Abuse Research Center
Harvard Medical School—McLean Hospital

Dorothy to the Wizard:

"I think you are a very bad man," said Dorothy.
"Oh no, my dear; I'm really a very good man; but I'm a very bad Wizard."
—from THE WIZARD OF OZ

Man is endowed with the gift of wizardry, a talent for discovery and invention. The discovery and invention of substances that change the way we feel and behave are among man's special accomplishments, and, like so many other products of our wizardry, these substances have the capacity to harm as well as to help. Psychoactive drugs can cause profound changes in the chemistry of the brain and other vital organs, and although their legitimate use can relieve pain and cure disease, their abuse leads in a tragic number of cases to destruction.

Consider alcohol — available to all and yet regarded with intense ambivalence from biblical times to the present day. The use of alcoholic beverages dates back to our earliest ancestors. Alcohol use and misuse became associated with the worship of gods and demons. One of the most powerful Greek gods was Dionysus, lord of fruitfulness and god of wine. The Romans adopted Dionysus but changed his name to Bacchus. Festivals and holidays associated with Bacchus celebrated the harvest and the origins of life. Time has blurred the images of the Bacchanalian festival, but the theme of drunkenness as a major part of celebration has survived the pagan gods and remains a familiar part of modern society. The term "Bacchanalian Festival" conveys a more appealing image than "drunken orgy" or "pot party," but whatever the label, drinking alcohol is a form of drug use that results in addiction for millions.

The fact that many millions of other people can use alcohol in moderation does not mitigate the toll this drug takes on society as a whole. According to reliable estimates, one out of every ten Americans develops a serious alcohol-related problem sometime in his or her lifetime. In addition, automobile accidents caused by drunken drivers claim the lives of tens of thousands every year. Many of the victims are gifted young people, just starting out in adult life. Hospital emergency rooms abound with patients seeking help for alcohol-related injuries.

Who is to blame? Can we blame the many manufacturers who produce such an amazing variety of alcoholic beverages? Should we blame the educators who fail to explain the perils of intoxication, or so exaggerate the dangers of drinking that no one could possibly believe them? Are friends to blame — those peers who urge others to "drink more and faster," or the macho types who stress the importance of being able to "hold your liquor"? Casting blame, however, is hardly constructive, and pointing the finger is a fruitless way to deal with the problem. Alcoholism and drug abuse have few culprits but many victims. Accountability begins with each of us, every time we choose to use or misuse an intoxicating substance.

It is ironic that some of man's earliest medicines, derived from natural plant products, are used today to poison and to intoxicate. Relief from pain and suffering is one of society's many continuing goals. Over 3,000 years ago, the Therapeutic Papyrus of Thebes, one of our earliest written records, gave instructions for the use of opium in the treatment of pain. Opium, in the form of its major derivative, morphine, and similar compounds, such as heroin, have also been used by many to induce changes in mood and feeling. Another example of man's misuse of a natural substance is the coca leaf, which for centuries was used by the Indians of Peru to reduce fatigue and hunger. Its modern derivative, cocaine, has important medical use as a local anesthetic. Unfortunately, its increasing abuse in the 1980s clearly has reached epidemic proportions.

The purpose of this series is to explore in depth the psychological and behavioral effects that psychoactive drugs have on the individual, and also, to investigate the ways in which drug use influences the legal, economic, cultural, and even moral aspects of societies. The information presented here (and in other books in this series) is based on many clinical and laboratory studies and other observations by people from diverse walks of life.

Over the centuries, novelists, poets, and dramatists have provided us with many insights into the sometimes seductive but ultimately problematic aspects of alcohol and drug use. Physicians, lawyers, biologists, psychologists, and social scientists have contributed to a better understanding of the causes and consequences of using these substances. The authors in this series have attempted to gather and condense all the latest information about drug use and abuse. They have also described the sometimes wide gaps in our knowledge and have suggested some new ways to answer many difficult questions.

One such question, for example, is how do alcohol and drug problems get started? And what is the best way to treat them when they do? Not too many years ago, alcoholics and drug abusers were regarded as evil, immoral, or both. It is now recognized that these persons suffer from very complicated diseases involving deep psychological and social problems. To understand how the disease begins and progresses, it is necessary to understand the nature of the substance, the behavior of addicts, and the characteristics of the society or culture in which they live.

Although many of the social environments we live in are very similar, some of the most subtle differences can strongly influence our thinking and behavior. Where we live, go to school and work, whom we discuss things with — all influence our opinions about drug use and misuse. Yet we also share certain commonly accepted beliefs that outweigh any differences in our attitudes. The authors in this series have tried to identify and discuss the central, most crucial issues concerning drug use and misuse.

Despite the increasing sophistication of the chemical substances we create in the laboratory, we have a long way to go in our efforts to make these powerful drugs work for us rather than against us.

The volumes in this series address a wide range of timely questions. What influence has drug use had on the arts? Why do so many of today's celebrities and star athletes use drugs, and what is being done to solve this problem? What is the relationship between drugs and crime? What is the physiological basis for the power drugs can hold over us? These are but a few of the issues explored in this far-ranging series.

Educating people about the dangers of drugs can go a long way towards minimizing the desperate consequences of substance abuse for individuals and society as a whole. Luckily, human beings have the resources to solve even the most serious problems that beset them, once they make the commitment to do so. As one keen and sensitive observer, Dr. Lewis Thomas, has said,

> There is nothing at all absurd about the human condition. We matter. It seems to me a good guess, hazarded by a good many people who have thought about it, that we may be engaged in the formation of something like a mind for the life of this planet. If this is so, we are still at the most primitive stage, still fumbling with language and thinking, but infinitely capacitated for the future. Looked at this way, it is remarkable that we've come as far as we have in so short a period, really no time at all as geologists measure time. We are the newest, youngest, and the brightest thing around.

CELEBRITY DRUG USE

Media attention is one of fame's mixed blessings. Rock star Madonna, who rejects drug use, has complained often and bitterly that constant hounding by the press undermines the quality of her private life.

AUTHOR'S PREFACE

Celebrities play a complex role in our society. Famous people are mobbed by the press as well as by adoring fans. They are instantly recognized by millions of people throughout the world, and the public's appetite for news of their lives is seemingly insatiable. But precisely because celebrities are so exposed, they frequently become scapegoats for weaknesses that pervade the entire society. Thus, if a famous figure falls victim to drug or alcohol abuse, his or her troubles are instantly exploited by a public that is as eager to rip down its idols as it is to build them up. In a sense, the heroes and villains of the media and the fan magazines are mere creatures of the culture that judges them.

It is in this light that *Celebrity Drug Use* should be read. Through historical perspectives and illustrative anecdotes this book explores the trials and tribulations of celebrities who, for one reason or another, have abused drugs, or responded to the problem of drug abuse in society.

The list of celebrities covered in this book is not exhaustive, but rather representative. No attempt has consciously been made to suggest the importance of celebrities by how much is written about them here, and no attempt is made to judge their morality, other than to note the destructive effects of drug abuse.

The author wishes to acknowledge with gratitude the assistance of Gary H. Grossman, coordinating producer of the television program "Entertainment Tonight," for his generous help in providing information, advice, and encouragement.

In the 1930s Harry J. Anslinger, the first federal commissioner for narcotics control, launched a campaign to publicize the dangers of marijuana in an attempt to make the use of the drug illegal.

CHAPTER 1

THE HISTORICAL PERSPECTIVE

According to an old adage, humans are different from animals because humans take drugs. The desire to change the way the mind experiences the world has been common among people of very different cultures over the centuries. The potential for being a drug abuser, then, is perhaps a consequence of being human.

Thus, it should surprise no one that drug abuse and addiction are not singularly characteristic of any particular economic, social, religious, political, or artistic group.

Some psychoactive drugs, such as alcohol, opium, and natural hallucinogens, were a part of human culture long before anyone began to keep records of such things. Likewise, notable personalities were indulging in one drug or another long before lists of their names were compiled.

The use of marijuana to alter consciousness has its roots in the ancient world. The Chinese medical treatise *Pen Ts'ao*, compiled in the first century C.E. (C.E. stands for Common Era and means the same as A.D.), contains a reference to *ma*, the Chinese word for cannabis. In about 1500 B.C.E. (Before Common Era) the Aryans invaded India, bringing with them their holy books, which contained tales of the discovery of marijuana by the god Siva.

Ancient India, in fact, was the first marijuana-oriented culture, according to Ernest L. Abel's book *Marijuana: The First Twelve Thousand Years*. Its use has extended into the modern era; bhang, a drink made from marijuana leaves, referred to in ancient Indian literature as the "food of the gods," is commonly consumed in 20th-century India.

In 1839 the British surgeon and chemist W. B. O'Shaughnessy introduced cannabis into Western medicine after working with the drug in India. Since then, marijuana has had a long and complex medical, social, and legal history in the Western world. Users of this drug have ranged from 19th-century Romantic writers to 20th-century jazz and rock musicians.

There have also been important figures involved with legislation concerning the use of marijuana. One of these people was Harry J. Anslinger, who became the first commissioner of the U.S. Treasury Department's Bureau of Narcotics in 1930. Anslinger, who had previously been assistant commissioner of Prohibition, (which, under the 18th constitutional amendment, in effect in the United States from 1920 to 1933, outlawed the sale and consumption of alcohol), believed that the best way to fight drug addiction was through strong laws, good enforcement, and stiff sentences. But he was reluctant at first to support antimarijuana measures. There were no federal laws under which marijuana offenses could be prosecuted, and enforcement of such laws would demand more staff time than he could spare. His attitude changed a couple of years later, however, after Congress, seeking to cut the federal budget during the height of the Depression, trimmed Anslinger's budget by $200,000 — a great deal of money in those days.

Anslinger responded by launching a major media campaign on the dangers and horrors of marijuana and by supplying information about the drug to press and community organizations. He even wrote an article for *American Magazine* in which he referred to marijuana as a narcotic "as dangerous as a coiled rattlesnake."

He also urged state legislatures that were considering passage of the Uniform State Narcotic Act to include marijuana on the list of drugs the bill would make illegal. At the time, the possession of drugs was not illegal. The Harrison Act of 1914, which was the major drug-control law in the country, was merely a tax measure designed to generate revenue from the legal sale of opiates to addicts.

In 1937 Anslinger was a major witness in the congressional hearings concerning the need to curb marijuana trafficking. Although no qualified experts on the drug testified, the congressional committee did hear excerpts from gruesome stories of the dangers of marijuana that had been printed in newspapers and magazines. Many of those stories, however, had been provided in the first place by Anslinger.

In his book on marijuana, Abel points out that at least some of the congressmen on the committee still were not sure what they were voting on even after the hearing. He cites the *Congressional Record* of the 81st Congress, 1st session, in which the following exchange between two lawmakers was recorded:

> *Mr. Snell*: What is the bill?
> *Mr. Rayburn*: It has something to do with something that is called marihuana [sic]. I believe it is a narcotic of some kind.

In 1937 Franklin D. Roosevelt became the first president to enact antimarijuana legislation. Called the Marijuana Tax Act, the new law curbed trafficking of the drug but did not directly prohibit its use.

In any case, the House passed the bill and sent it to the Senate, which also passed it and returned it to the House for final action. The House sent it on to President Franklin Roosevelt, who signed it on August 3, 1937.

Concern about marijuana use continued to grow during the next two decades, and new, even tougher laws were passed. Again, Anslinger was called to testify before the congressional committees considering these bills.

Along the way, however, some studies cast doubt on the reputation of marijuana as a dangerous narcotic that drove its users to acts of sex, sex abuse, sadistic criminal acts, and heroin addiction. One such study was the "LaGuardia Report," which was published in 1944 by a team of New York scientists. The "LaGuardia Report" concluded that although marijuana lowered inhibitions it did not lead to aggressive behavior.

Beat poet Allen Ginsberg (foreground) and followers participate in an anti–Vietnam War protest. During the late 1960s and early 1970s, Ginsberg was outspoken about his approval of marijuana use.

By the 1960s, of course, marijuana had moved out of the realm of minority neighborhoods and jazz halls and onto the college campuses of middle-class America. When marijuana-smoking students from respectable families began to run afoul of the law over marijuana, the laws began to ease. By the 1970s, some states had reduced marijuana possession to a misdemeanor.

Needless to say, cultural attitudes toward marijuana changed radically in the years between Harry Anslinger's heyday and the development of the counterculture of the late 1960s and early 1970s. In 1966, Allen Ginsberg, one of the best-known of the Beat poets, wrote an article on marijuana, a portion of which appeared in *The Atlantic* magazine. Titled "The Great Marijuana Hoax," it was Ginsberg's manifesto to end what he considered the myths about marijuana that antidrug activists were spreading. "The black cloud of negative propaganda," Ginsberg wrote, "emanates from one particular source: the U.S. Treasury Department Narcotics Bureau."

Ginsberg discussed his own experiences under the influence of marijuana, stressing that the drug gave him fresh insights into "certain pieces of jazz and classical music" as well as the work of various painters.

Ginsberg, who was awarded the 1986 Frost Medal for distinguished poetic achievement by the Poetry Society of America, was outspoken in support of a person's right to smoke marijuana. This stance sometimes made him a target of law-enforcement officials. For example, he wrote that he was extensively searched by customs agents when he returned from a trip to Europe. The agents analyzed the dust from his pockets, he wrote, for the presence of marijuana.

In 1966 Ginsberg told an audience at a poetry reading in Paterson, New Jersey, that he had smoked marijuana while looking at the Passaic Falls the day before, in order to "bring out the full meaning of the episode," according to the *New York Times*. In response to newspaper articles and phone calls about Ginsberg's statement, the mayor of Paterson ordered police to arrest the poet if they could prove that he had actually smoked marijuana at the Falls.

In 1972 Ginsberg and other noted figures, including the radical activist and attorney William Kunstler, were among those who lobbied for the suspension of the jail sentence of poet John Sinclair, who was arrested for possession of two

Jack Ford, son of former President Gerald R. Ford, admitted that he had smoked marijuana and stated that he believed the law should restrict, but not outlaw, use of the drug.

marijuana cigarettes. Sinclair had been sentenced by a Detroit court to 9½ to 10 years in prison and served 29 months before the Michigan Supreme Court reversed his conviction. Two of the justices held that Sinclair's sentence was cruel and unusual punishment, and one justice held that the poet had been entrapped by Detroit police.

Another incident that reflected the lenient attitudes during the 1970s concerning the use of marijuana involved an article in the Portland, Oregon, newspaper *Oregonian*. It was reported that President Gerald R. Ford's 23-year-old son Jack had smoked marijuana. The younger Ford also said he believed that the law should treat marijuana as it does beer and wine.

"I've smoked marijuana before," he said, "and I don't think that's so exceptional for people growing up in the 1960s."

Ford said that he did not use hard drugs, and he worried that his associations with people who did use hard drugs would hurt his father's election campaign.

The following year Jeff Carter, the then 22-year-old son of the Democratic presidential candidate Jimmy Carter, confirmed the assertion of his mother, Rosalynn, that he had tried marijuana. But he also said, "I don't recommend it to anybody."

Mrs. Carter had disclosed in an earlier interview that her three sons had all smoked marijuana. In confirming his mother's disclosure, Jeff Carter added, "I don't know why she said it. I kind of wish she hadn't."

Five years later, Edward M. Kennedy, Jr., and another student at Wesleyan University in Middletown, Connecticut, were stopped for speeding in New Jersey by a state trooper who found marijuana in their car. A municipal court judge granted Kennedy a conditional discharge on misdemeanor charges of possession of less than 25 grams of marijuana and fined him $15 for speeding.

Although the fates of these children of important political figures illustrate the trend toward leniency regarding marijuana misdemeanors, the tide may very well be turning. Research conducted in the 1980s has resulted in increasing evidence regarding the dangerous effects of marijuana. These discoveries may in turn lead to stricter consequences for those convicted of possession of the drug.

South American Indians inhabiting the Andes Mountains have cultivated the coca plant, *Erythroxylum coca*, for many hundreds of years. The rural workers in Bolivia and Peru, especially, still chew coca leaves daily to help them cope with life in the high altitudes, where work is hard and food is scarce.

In 1862 the German chemist Albert Niemann isolated the active ingredient in coca leaves, an alkaloid substance that he called cocaine. He noted that the substance produced an anesthetic effect that made the tongue temporarily insensitive to touch.

The famous Viennese psychiatrist Sigmund Freud used cocaine, and in 1884 wrote a medical paper "Über Coca" ("About Coca") which proposed that cocaine be regarded as a stimulant like caffeine, rather than as a narcotic like opium. He recommended that physicians prescribe it, claiming that it could treat narcotic addiction. In fact, Freud himself pre-

The founder of modern psychoanalysis, the Viennese physician Sigmund Freud was at first enthusiastic about the therapeutic use of cocaine. But when a close friend died of its effects, Freud was forced to acknowledge the drug's destructive potential.

scribed cocaine to treat his friend Ernst Von Fleischl-Marxow, a morphine addict. Tragically, Fleischl-Marxow began using cocaine excessively and ultimately died of its effects. Although Freud did not cease his use of cocaine for many years, he did begin to write about the newly discovered dangers of the drug.

Also in the 1880s, a Corsican chemist named Angelo Mariani used this coca extract in a wine called Vin Mariani. It became an immensely popular medicine for fatigue, nervousness, and a variety of other ills. Mariani sent free samples to celebrities and solicited their endorsements.

Among the public figures who sang the praises of Vin Mariani were Pope Leo XIII, the inventor Thomas Edison, and former U.S. president Ulysses S. Grant. The Scottish author Robert Louis Stevenson is said to have been inspired by cocaine while writing his famous novel *The Strange Case of Dr. Jekyll and Mr. Hyde.* And Sir Arthur Conan Doyle, the creator of the fictional detective Sherlock Holmes, was a physician acquainted with the ways of cocaine. Doyle portrayed Holmes as an occasional heavy user of cocaine. Although aware that the drug was bad for him, the detective injected it because cocaine was "transcendentally stimulating and clarifying to the mind."

Mariani faced stiff competition in the cocaine marketplace as the use of cocaine and cocaine tonics burgeoned. In 1886, an Atlanta, Georgia, soda fountain began dispensing Dr. John Styth Pemberton's "brain cola." Called Coca-Cola, it was a mixture of carbonated water and coca-laced syrup. It hit the market in bottles in 1894. Coca-Cola also faced competition from tonics with names such as Koca Nola, Celery Cola, Wiseola, and even Dope Cola. But by 1903, government concern over the dangers of drugs in soft drinks led to regulations that forced the companies to remove cocaine from their sodas. Congress prohibited most importation of coca leaves and

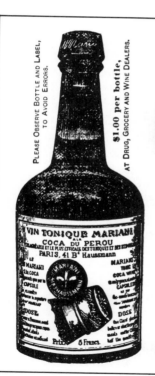

For Body and Brain.

SINCE 30 YEARS ALL EMINENT PHYSICIANS RECOMMEND

VIN MARIANI

The original French Coca Wine; most popularly used tonic-stimulant in *Hospitals, Public and Religious Institutions* everywhere.

Nourishes Fortifies Refreshes

Strengthens entire system; most AGREEABLE, EFFECTIVE and LASTING Renovator of the Vital Forces.

Every test, strictly on its own merits, will prove its exceptional reputation.

PALATABLE AS CHOICEST OLD WINES.

Illustrated Book Sent Free, address:

MARIANI & CO., NEW YORK

TRIAL WILL CONVINCE

An 1893 advertisement for Vin Mariani. This wine, immensely popular in the late 19th century and endorsed by several prominent public figures, was one of several preparations that contained cocaine.

cocaine into the United States in 1922; by the end of 1931, every state had instituted severe criminal sanctions against the use of cocaine, except for medical purposes. Once supply dwindled, the price of illegal cocaine shot up, and it became a rich person's drug.

By the 1930s, horror stories about cocaine in magazines and on the screen began to explore rather dramatically the dangers of this drug. Cocaine entered the realm of songwriters, too. In 1934 the composer and lyricist Cole Porter wrote in one of his songs, "I get no kick from cocaine . . . "

By the 1970s, however, the demand for cocaine had grown once again, and a savage underworld of "cocaine cowboys" slaughtered each other in an effort to wrest control of the lucrative cocaine distribution network that supplied American recreational users and addicts.

Not surprisingly, celebrity names began turning up in newspapers, in magazines, and on the evening news, as this fashionable "drug of choice" attracted users and dealers among the ranks of public figures and their children. One such celebrity was Abbie Hoffman, a 1960s political figure who helped form the protest group known as the Youth International Party (YIP, whose members were called Yippies). Hoffman was arrested in 1968 and charged with organizing violent demonstrations at the Democratic National Convention. In 1973 he was arrested in New York for selling cocaine. The following year Hoffman failed to appear in state supreme court to face those charges and, instead, went underground, living for a while in South America and Europe. He turned himself in to face the drug charges in 1980 after surfacing in a resort area of upstate New York. He had been living there for several years under the alias of Barry Freed, and had been working as an environmental activist.

Hoffman served a few years in jail and in work-release programs. By 1986 Hoffman was, at age 50, the host of a weekly FM radio talk show, *Radio Free USA*, carried by the New York City station WBAI.

According to a United Press International report, Hoffman used his first show to enter the 1980s debate on whether employers concerned about drug use among employees should force their workers to submit to urine tests, an idea supported by President Ronald Reagan. "We don't think Americans should be judged by the contents of a Dixie cup," Hoffman said.

In 1982 car mogul John DeLorean was accused of financing a $24-million cocaine deal. DeLorean was acquitted, but his case highlighted the fact that cocaine use is widespread among professionals.

Another widely publicized incident concerning the illicit use of cocaine involved John Z. DeLorean, a former head of General Motors and the founder of a Northern Ireland company that manufactured the DeLorean sports car.

DeLorean was arrested by undercover agents in 1982 on charges of financing a cocaine deal in order to raise money to help his financially ailing company. DeLorean was acquitted, but his trial highlighted the pervasive use of cocaine among some of the nation's most prominent professionals, as well as its "stars."

As with marijuana, cocaine has its share of victims among children of respected celebrities. In 1983 John V. Lindsay, Jr., the then 23-year-old son of the former mayor of New York City, was sentenced to six months in jail after pleading guilty to selling cocaine to an undercover police officer. United Press International reported that as the younger Lindsay was being led out of the courtroom in handcuffs, his father sat in the rear of the room shaking his head.

The following year David Anthony Kennedy, one of the sons of the late Senator Robert F. Kennedy, was found dead in his Palm Beach, Florida, apartment. He had been a patient at several drug rehabilitation centers in the past, and friends said he was depressed after reading an unflattering excerpt from a book about his family. Traces of cocaine and Demerol were found in his bloodstream. His problem with drugs could well have had its roots, at least in part, in the shock of seeing his father assassinated on television during the 1968 Democratic presidential campaign.

Two years later, John A. Zaccaro, Jr., the son of Geraldine A. Ferraro, the 1984 Democratic vice-presidential candidate, was arrested at a restaurant in Middlebury, Vermont, where he worked as a bartender, on charges of selling a quarter-gram of cocaine to an undercover police officer in his off-campus apartment. Zaccaro, who was attending Middlebury College at the time, pleaded not guilty to charges of possession with intent to sell and the sale of a regulated drug. The following month he withdrew from the college.

In 1938, a Swiss chemist named Albert Hofmann synthesized the hallucinogenic compound LSD in his laboratory at Sandoz Laboratory in Basel, Switzerland. After accidentally inhaling some of the powder while preparing a sample for animal experiments to test the drug's ability to cause uterine contractions, Hofmann became sick, dizzy, and restless. Three days later, in order to confirm it was indeed the LSD that had caused his symptoms, he took one quarter of a milligram of LSD orally before going home. The amount he consumed was five times the effective dose of 0.05 milligram. Approximately 40 minutes after ingesting the drug, Hofmann was in turmoil and felt dizziness, visual disturbances, a tendency to laugh at inappropriate times, and difficulty concentrating. Hofmann's experience lasted approximately six hours and may well have been the first bad LSD "trip."

By the early 1960s, two Harvard University psychologists, Dr. Timothy Leary and Dr. Richard Alpert, were promoting the use of "consciousness-expanding" drugs, such as LSD, psilocybin, and mescaline. They performed experiments on students, and eventually Leary set up a quasi-religious community extolling the virtues of these drugs. He was later arrested on drug charges and jailed during the 1970s.

On the West Coast, writer Ken Kesey was holding "acid tests" during which volunteers partook of LSD in a partylike atmosphere complete with music and flashing lights. The source of much of the LSD consumed, especially on the West Coast, was the "laboratory" of Augustus Owsley Stanley III, the so-called King of LSD. He was arrested in 1969 for manufacturing the drug and spent two-and-a-half years in a federal prison. Freed on parole in December 1972, he was arrested again on the same charge the following year, in addition to being indicted for income-tax evasion.

Also in 1969, the year of Stanley's first arrest, Diane Linkletter, the 20-year-old daughter of television personality Art Linkletter, took LSD to combat her depression after having a quarrel with her boyfriend. Under the influence of the drug, she jumped from the kitchen window of her sixth-floor apartment in Los Angeles.

"It wasn't a suicide," her distraught father later told the *Los Angeles Times*, "because she wasn't herself. It was murder. She was murdered by the people who manufacture and sell LSD."

Dr. Timothy Leary, a former professor at Harvard University, experimented heavily with LSD during the 1960s and urged thousands of students to "turn on, tune in, drop out." Leary was eventually arrested and jailed on drug charges.

A few weeks later, in an effort to drum up support for his antidrug program, President Richard Nixon invited Linkletter to address a White House meeting of congressional leaders and other officials on the subject of his daughter's death. During that 1969 meeting, according to the *New York Times*, Linkletter suggested that the government and private groups should begin a program on the dangers of drug abuse aimed at children in the elementary grades. He also refused to blame children for the growing incidence of drug abuse.

"In this world of frustrations," Linkletter said, "children turn to the only thing they have known since they were born — they are used to seeing people pop chemicals into their mouths for everything from relieving tensions and curing headaches to losing weight."

But Linkletter did criticize the entertainment industry for "unwittingly tempting young people into the world of drugs," according to the *Times*. "Almost every time a top-40 record is played on the radio," he said, "it is an ad for acid, marijuana and trips. The lyrics of the popular songs and the jackets on the albums . . . are all a complete, total campaign for the fun and thrill of trips.

"If you don't believe it, you ought to take a good, long look at some of the lyrics and some of the albums with the hidden symbols, with the language that the kids know."

Linkletter's statements were echoed over a decade later as parents began to level charges that the record industry in the 1980s was encouraging drug use, as well as sex and violence, in the songs being sung by popular groups.

In 1806, the German chemist Friedrich Wilhelm Adam Serteurner isolated morphine, the active ingredient in opium, and reported that he "got into a dreamy state" after testing it on himself.

In 1898, the German chemist Heinrich Dreser, director of the Bayer Company in Darmstadt, Germany, prepared diacetylmorphine, a derivative of morphine, and called it heroin. Ironically, the new drug was quickly marketed as a safer and quicker pain reliever than morphine. Although morphine and heroin found a place in the medical arsenal in the battle against pain, both drugs soon proved to be both highly addictive and subject to serious abuse.

Taken in excess, morphine is one of many drugs that can be lethal. According to an article published in 1986 in the journal *History Today*, the toxic (poisonous) properties of morphine were used in 1936 to hasten the death of King George V of England. In failing health for several months with a chronic bronchial disorder, the king rapidly grew weaker in the final days of his life. With the king near death, his doctor, Lord Dawson, feared that his royal patient would not die until after midnight, too late for his death to be announced in the prestigious morning newspaper. That was considered to be a more appropriate forum for such eventful news than the afternoon tabloids.

He also believed that the king should not linger near death for hours, perhaps in discomfort, but rather that he should die quickly, "with the dignity and the serenity which he so richly merited and which demanded a brief final scene," according to the notes the physician made after the king's death.

Therefore, at about 11:00 P.M. on the evening of January 20, 1936, in Sandringham Castle, Lord Dawson gave the king two injections, consisting of three-quarters of a gram of morphine and one gram of cocaine. Less than an hour later, the king died, and the announcement made the morning paper, which ran the headline "A Peaceful Ending at Midnight."

Almost 50 years after the king's death by injection, Charles James Spencer-Churchill, the great-nephew of Sir Winston Churchill, Britain's great leader during World War II, was convicted in an English court of breaking into a pharmacy in search of heroin, and for the possession of heroin found in his car. He was fined and placed on probation in 1985.

Needless to say, the children of American celebrities have not been spared the unwanted publicity that hounds the famous and the powerful when they are in trouble.

On September 11, 1983, Robert Kennedy, Jr., another son of Senator Robert Kennedy and David Kennedy's older brother, entered Fair Oaks Hospital, a drug-treatment center in Summit, New Jersey, for treatment of his heroin addiction. Kennedy had become ill a few days before on an airplane flight to Rapid City, South Dakota.

Authorities there confiscated his flight bag to look for drugs. By the time Kennedy entered Fair Oaks, South Dakota

Robert F. Kennedy, Jr., the oldest son of the late senator, was arrested for possession of heroin in 1984. Subsequent medical treatment enabled him to overcome his dependence.

authorities had determined that Kennedy's bag contained a small amount of heroin, and a warrant was subsequently issued for his arrest.

The following February, Kennedy returned to South Dakota to plead guilty to possession of two-tenths of a gram of heroin. At the time he was undergoing six months of postrelease treatment for his drug problem and was working as a volunteer for a legal fund devoted to environmental concerns.

In March 1984 Kennedy was sentenced to two years' probation and ordered to take periodic tests for drug use, join a support group called Narcotics Anonymous, and perform 1,500 hours of community service.

Kennedy's drug problem had threatened to derail a promising future as a lawyer. An adventurer who had done white-water rafting on the roaring rivers of South America, skied down the slopes of the Andes Mountains, and appeared in an African wildlife documentary, Kennedy also sought the adventures of drugs; he abused alcohol, cocaine, Valium, and finally, heroin.

Despite his drug problems, Kennedy had managed to graduate from law school, but he failed his bar exams. Meanwhile, young acquaintances seeking his friendship repeatedly supplied him with drugs. Although he had tried to kick his drug habit, he feared the publicity that would attend his admission to treatment. Fortunately, once Kennedy finally did obtain the help he needed, he was able to put his life back on track. He passed his bar exams and was admitted to the New York State bar in June 1985.

For many years, "respectable" middle-class America was able to write off drug abuse as a manifestation of moral weakness among the poor, the criminal, and the antisocial. By the end of the 20th century, of course, this reassuring self-delusion can no longer be supported. If anything, patterns of illicit drug use seem to be set now by elites, whether in business, politics, or entertainment. In the following chapters, we will explore some of the specifics and the consequences of this phenomenon.

Rock star Janis Joplin in concert. One of the most successful recording artists of the 1960s, Joplin became addicted to heroin and alcohol and died of a heroin overdose in 1970.

CHAPTER 2

THE MUSIC WORLD

Perhaps nowhere else in the entertainment industry has the use of drugs been so pervasive as in the music business. Musical artists have turned to illicit drugs in a misguided quest for heightened creativity and performance. Singers and musicians have turned to substance abuse to escape the misery of faded careers. Sadly, many members of the music world have indulged in drugs for purely "recreational" reasons. And, in fact, drugs have ended not only the careers but the lives of some noted musical artists.

The link between drug use and modern American music has its roots in turn-of-the-century New Orleans, the birthplace of the first purely American form of music — jazz. Some jazz musicians discovered that marijuana slowed down their perception of time, and that this illusion helped them to improvise. For this reason marijuana became very popular among jazz artists.

The attitudes of jazz musicians toward marijuana were extremely positive and in fact lighthearted, but it and other drugs began to take their toll among musicians and singers.

For example the drummer Gene Krupa, one of the leading jazz musicians of his time, was arrested for possession of marijuana in 1941 and served an 84-day sentence in a San

Francisco jail. In 1969 Krupa spoke before a group of youths in Mineola, Long Island, telling them how his use of marijuana almost ruined his career.

"I thought it would better my playing," he told his young audience, "but that was a hallucination. The first thing that marijuana does is distort time, and time is the essence to a drummer." Krupa said that he knew of at least 100 very talented musicians whose careers had been ruined by the use of drugs.

Another popular drug among jazz musicians was alcohol, which had been a classic drug and abused for centuries. One of the early jazz greats to succumb to alcohol was Leon Bismarck ("Bix") Beiderbecke. Born in Davenport, Iowa, in 1903, Bix was a driven artist, known for his brilliant cornet playing. He recorded with some of the giants of the jazz world, including Hoagy Carmichael, Benny Goodman, Jimmy Dorsey, and Gene Krupa.

The French Quarter of New Orleans, the birthplace of jazz. Many jazz musicians used marijuana in the mistaken belief that it could enhance creativity.

Drummer Gene Krupa (right) improvises with fellow musician Benny Goodman. Krupa, whose use of marijuana almost ruined his career in the 1940s, later spoke out on the dangers of the drug.

But Bix was also an unhappy, restless man who changed jobs often and drank heavily. Drinking eventually hurt his performance, and by 1931 his professional life was just about over.

According to *The Jazz Book* by Joachim E. Berendt, frustration appeared to push Bix to the bottle. Berendt quotes trumpeter Jimmy McPartland, who was close to Bix: "I think one of the reasons he drank so much was that he was a perfectionist and wanted to do more with music than any man possibly could."

Ironically, Bix in fact crippled his own musical talents with alcohol. His health ruined, he could not make it back into the big time. Yet he pushed himself into playing a job one night, and the effort taxed his frail body beyond its limits. Bix developed a severe cold that turned into pneumonia, and on August 7, 1931, he died at the age of 28.

By the 1940s "bebop" jazz had arrived, and with it came that musical form's more elaborate rhythm structure and focus on harmony rather than melody. It was at this point that another drug entered the world of jazz. That drug was heroin. Pushers found a willing clientele among some jazz musicians as well as jazz and popular music singers, some of whom ended up in jail, addicted, or dead. The increasing number of drug overdose related deaths became a tragic roll call.

Charlie "Bird" Parker, who, with his brilliant improvisations on saxophone became one of the leaders of bebop, is said to have commented that he never played better than when he was "cold sober." Nonetheless, he became addicted to heroin and died in 1955 at the age of 35.

One of the luckier artists of this era was Dexter Gordon, who became what many fans and critics would consider the first bebop tenor saxophonist. Gordon became a heroin addict, was arrested several times, and spent time in prison. Gordon later spent 14 years as an expatriate jazz musician in Europe, returning to the United States in the 1970s. At the time he left, jazz musicians tended to receive more enthusiastic receptions in Europe than in America. In addition, musicians convicted of drug offenses generally lost their cabaret cards — licenses that permitted them to perform in New York, a major market for their skills.

In 1960, Gordon worked with a Los Angeles experimental theater production called *The Connection*, which took a harsh, realistic look at a group of heroin addicts. Gordon not only appeared in it as a musician but also composed the score.

Gordon also starred in *'Round Midnight*, a 1986 film about a jazz musician who, reminiscent of Gordon himself, is an expatriate saxophonist living in Paris. (Gordon received a Best Actor Academy nomination for his performance.) During an interview that year, which was published in *Rolling Stone* magazine, Gordon recounted his early days in New York, when heroin was commonly used among his fellow musicians, and the terrible experience of addiction.

"In our peer group," he said, "it became an acceptable social happenstance. But also understand this: we didn't know, we didn't understand what it was. This wasn't marijuana, right? I mean grass, if you got it, all right; if you *don't* have it all right. Of course, with heroin, it came, and it was

Dexter Gordon, a brilliant and successful jazz saxophonist, was plagued by heroin addiction during the 1950s but was able to overcome his habit and resume his career.

groovy. I mean, great feeling, man. Later, when it became mandatory, daily, twenty-four hours, then you begin to realize —ohh, ——."

In addition to its destructive effects among musicians, the specter of drugs haunted the lives of some of the great vocalists who interpreted the current jazz and pop music of the last several decades.

Bessie Smith, called the "Empress of the Blues," was the favorite singer of the jazz-listening public during the 1920s and made lasting impressions on such jazz artists as Bix Beiderbecke and Benny Goodman. Her renditions of such blues classics as "Weeping Willow Blues" and "St. Louis Blues" were among the most popular recordings of the time.

But changing popular tastes eventually caused her popularity to decline. Already a drinker, Smith became an alcoholic during the last years of her life. She died in 1937 in an auto accident while on tour in Mississippi.

Eleanora Fagan was another gifted jazz singer, better known by her legendary stage name, Billie Holiday. Born in a Baltimore ghetto in 1915, Holiday changed her name in an attempt to rise above her past, which she loathed. She was, of course, to become one of the great interpreters of songs during the 1940s and 1950s. Along the way she paid her dues, quitting school in the fifth grade to help support her family and singing for all-night parties in after-hours clubs when she was 15. And always there were the memories of the violent racism she had witnessed, and of course the lure of drugs.

Like many other jazz artists, she became addicted to heroin. Her biographer and friend, William Duffy, wrote that she may have turned to heroin in part because the drug helped her believe she had found the truth as she wished it had been.

Drugs helped her forget, but drugs also got her sent to prison in 1947; she was arrested again in 1949 on drug-possession charges but was acquitted and released.

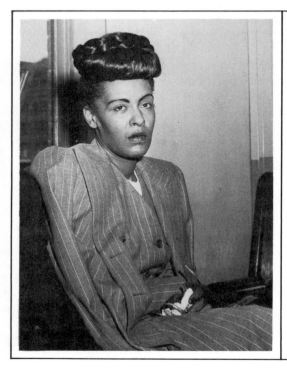

Billie Holiday sits in a police station after being arrested on drug charges. Holiday was perhaps the greatest female jazz vocalist of all time, but abuse of drugs and alcohol eventually took its toll on her voice; the results are evident in her last recordings.

She continued to sing but remained a heroin addict for the rest of her life. The rough, highly emotional quality of her singing had won her a legion of fans, and many of them attended the 44-year-old singer's funeral in July 1959.

While Holiday was mesmerizing audiences in the United States, another popular singer was reducing listeners to tears in Paris with her heart-rending songs of lost love and frustrated romance.

Edith Giovanna Gassion, who eventually became known as Edith Piaf, was born in 1915 in an impoverished Paris ghetto. Her father, Louis, was an acrobatic street performer; her mother, Anetta, sang songs in cheap music halls and cafes in the Montmartre section of Paris.

While Louis was fighting in World War I, Anetta abandoned the newborn Edith, leaving her with Edith's grandmother. The grandmother seldom bathed her little granddaughter and regularly laced the water in her baby bottle with wine, supposedly to kill germs.

When Edith's father came home from the war he rescued his little daughter from this squalor and brought her to live with his own mother, who ran a brothel in Normandy. When Edith was not quite seven, her father took her away to share his vagabond life. They traveled together from town to town, and Louis performed for what money he could get. They slept in dirty hotels or on the street. Edith sometimes joined her father in his acts, and she sang on the street for the first time when she was ten. When she was 15, she left her father and struck out on her own.

Edith later said of this time, "I was hungry, I was cold. But I was also free ... free not to get up in the morning, not to go to bed at night, free to get drunk if I liked, to dream ... to hope."

She developed the "street smarts" of a poor, desperate child who has learned to hustle to survive. When she was 16 Edith fell in love with a young man. The relationship broke up, and the daughter born from their affair died in infancy from meningitis.

Stunned, depressed, and feeling guilty at her inability to care for the child, Edith left the menial job she held at that time and began to sing for money outside cafes and in dance halls.

Edith Piaf performs at a New York nightclub. Piaf, whose early death was caused partly by morphine addiction, reflected the tragedy and sadness of her own life in many of her songs.

When Edith was 22 a cabaret owner invited her to perform in his establishment. He changed her last name to Piaf, which means "little sparrow." Piaf quickly became a favorite of the customers, and her career blossomed. But disaster continued to haunt her.

After World War II, during which she sang only for prisoners of war, Piaf fell in love with a boxer named Marcel Cerdan. Tragically, Cerdan died two years later in a plane crash. Piaf then married singer Jacques Pills in 1952, but was divorced five years later.

In addition to these traumatic relationships, Piaf suffered from illnesses that wracked her body regularly in her later years, from injuries she sustained in two automobile accidents, and from the pain of rheumatism.

Piaf had been a heavy drinker for years, and the accidents and rheumatism left a legacy of pain that she treated with morphine. Although she fought morphine addiction on occasion, she was addicted for much of her adult life.

Haunted by her past and hounded by tragedy and pain, Piaf suffused her singing with a genuine emotion that profoundly touched her fans. But all the drinking, the drugs, and her own demanding schedule caught up with her in January 1959 during a performance in New York. Piaf collapsed on stage and was taken to a hospital, where she underwent an operation for stomach ulcers and internal bleeding. She reduced her drug use for a while after that but never became completely drug-free.

By 1963, she had taxed her body beyond its limits. That year she spent eight weeks in a hospital in suburban Paris recovering from a serious illness. Six months later, she died in her home in the south of France at the age of 48.

While Piaf was singing of lost love in Parisian nightclubs during the 1950s, exciting things were happening on the other side of the Atlantic Ocean. In the United States, the musical juggernaut of rock and roll was gaining the momentum that would help make it a major, influential form of music.

One of the leaders of this new trend was the black singer and musician Richard Wayne Penniman, better known as Little Richard. Born to a very religious family in Macon, Georgia, Little Richard became a rock star in 1955 when he recorded "Tutti Frutti," one of the biggest hits of the decade. The song was significant because it was popular among not only black people but white fans as well.

The following year Little Richard recorded his next hit, the immortal "Long Tall Sally." As one hit followed another, more white artists were influenced by Little Richard, and the young man from Macon, Georgia, became an important star.

Little Richard did something else, too. With his high pompadour hairstyle, his sometimes shrill but always powerful voice, his manic movements, high energy, driving beat, makeup, and flamboyant outfits, he turned a generation of rock-and-roll listeners into frenzied fans.

Little Richard's fans shouted at concerts. They screamed. They jumped up and wailed. They charged the stage. And girls swooned for this pulsating, sweating, outrageous figure, screaming out his sometimes sexually suggestive lyrics.

This horrified many parents, as the actions of another rock-and-roll pioneer, Elvis Presley, would later do. In addition, white acceptance of this high-profile black entertainer shocked and angered many segregationists. Although white kids had been listening to black rhythm-and-blues and rock-and-roll musicians for some time, the adulation of Little Richard was unprecedented.

Rock and roll was beginning to break the rules of propriety, segregation, and sexual restraint. As well as being a new musical movement, it signaled the onset of a rebellious change in the attitudes of America's youth toward authority and the establishment. Part of that rebellion would include

One of the pioneers of rock music during the 1950s, Little Richard later almost destroyed himself with drugs. He was able to make a comeback, however, once he solved his substance-abuse problems.

Years after his death Elvis Presley remains an icon for millions of fans. Tragically, his notorious abuse of prescription drugs eroded the talent that had rocketed him to stardom; his last years were scarred by addiction.

drug use and abuse. Among the many casualties of that rebellion would be the musical artists who took drugs. Some lived through it, others burned themselves out or died.

Little Richard was one of these musicians who experimented heavily with drugs.

"It started in the quiet gloom of a recording studio, at a long session, sandwiched between one-night stands that were 300 miles apart," wrote author Charles White, in his biography, *The Life and Times of Little Richard*. "They were all tired. Drained. But time was money. So when the man laid the white powder on the table, they sniffed and found instant euphoria and the energy to do four more takes." The cocaine eased fatigue and gave Little Richard and his band "a rush of raw energy" that swept them through their grueling schedule. "But coke is no joke," White wrote. "The pleasure became the problem — maintaining the habit, and fighting off the mood swings and facing the dark side of the come-downs."

As Little Richard's career roared along, his drug problem slowly squeezed him in a chemical vise. He spent thousands of dollars on drugs, began to miss shows, and eventually ran out of money.

"They shoulda called me Little Cocaine, I was sniffing so much of the stuff," White quotes Little Richard as saying of himself during that time. "My nose got big enough to back a diesel truck in, unload it, and drive it right out again. Every time I blew my nose there was flesh and blood on my handkerchief, where it had eaten out my membranes."

He had gone from marijuana to PCP, cocaine, narcotics, and alcohol. The double strain of overwork and drugs ravaged his stomach; an early, erroneous diagnosis of stomach cancer caused a brief sensation in the press.

He was overwrought, sometimes paranoid, and could feel himself degenerating. Little Richard knew it was time to get his life under control. He left the rock scene in 1957, and, claiming that he had seen a vision of the Apocalypse, became an ordained minister in the Seventh-Day Adventist Church. Little Richard came back to the rock fold in 1964, but by then it was dominated by the new sound of the Beatles. He found work during the 1970s but never regained his superstar status. In 1979 he recorded an album of gospel songs; in 1986, after saying that he believed that music and rhythm were created by God, announced that he would begin a national tour the following year.

Little Richard was able to overcome his drug addiction and resume his career. His contemporary Elvis Presley was not quite so lucky. Presley, who was born in Memphis, Tennessee, and was a truck driver before he turned to music, became legendary in the 1950s as he recorded one gigantic hit after another. As his fame increased, however, so did his appetite for drugs.

Presley's physician, Dr. George Nichopolous, was investigated after the singer died in 1977. Although the medical examiner ruled that Presley died of cardiac arrythmia, a condition in which the heart beats irregularly, traces of many prescription drugs were found in his body: codeine, methaqualone, barbiturates, the tranquilizers Placidyl and Valium, the painkillers Demerol and Meperidine, morphine, and the antihistamine chlorpheniramine. It was discovered that Dr. Nichopolous had prescribed over 10,000 pills for Presley during the 2 years prior to the singer's death.

In his testimony, Dr. Nichopoulos said that the singer popped pills "from the time he woke up in the morning until the time he went to sleep at night," and that Presley was probably addicted to Demerol and barbiturates. Some physicians believed that certain drugs the singer took that night might have interacted with each other to produce a fatal effect. Regardless of how he died, Presley ended his extraordinary career as an obese and drug-dependent man.

In light of Presley's outrageous appetite for drugs of abuse, it is ironic that in 1970 the singer asked President Richard M. Nixon to make him a federal drug-enforcement agent. Presley explained that he could help the president's war on drugs because young people, including drug-using hippies, would accept him into their circles.

"I have done an in-depth study of drug abuse and Communist brainwashing techniques and I am right in the middle of the whole thing where I can and will do the most good," Presley had written in a letter to the president. Presley received a specially prepared badge, but no law-enforcement authority.

The 1960s witnessed the drug-related demises of a number of gifted musicians. This decade was marked not only by the social upheavals precipitated by opposition to America's participation in the Vietnam War, but by a growing abuse of such dangerous drugs as LSD and heroin. The rock music of the 1960s mirrored the preoccupations of the nation's youth, with lyrics that were antiwar, antiestablishment, and prodrug. A body of music that played on the visual and auditory distortions associated with hallucinogenic drugs was labeled "acid rock."

The Beatles' hit song "Lucy in the Sky with Diamonds" was widely taken as a depiction of an LSD "trip," though the singers themselves denied this. The Rolling Stones pitched in with "She's a Rainbow," the Amboy Dukes sang "Journey to the Center of Your Mind," and the Temptations recorded "Psychedelic Shack." Eric Burdon and the Animals sang "A Girl Named Sandoz," the name being an apparent reference to Sandoz Laboratory in Basel, Switzerland, where LSD was first synthesized.

Another group derived its very name from the early literature on hallucinogens. In 1964, an intelligent but brooding young man named Jim Morrison was studying theater arts at the University of California, Los Angeles. He was also dreaming of forming a band. He could not play an instrument or dance, and he did not even have a song to sing. But he had a name for the band that had its roots in a poem by the 19th-century writer William Blake. In Blake's "The Marriage of Heaven and Hell," the poet wrote of opening the "doors of perception." In the 20th century, Aldous Huxley described his experiences with the hallucinogenic drug mescaline in a book whose title, *The Doors of Perception*, was based on that phrase. Morrison picked it up from Huxley, and his band had a name.

Jim Morrison (center), lead singer of the rock group the Doors, named the band after Aldous Huxley's book Doors of Perception, *which chronicled Huxley's experience with psychedelic drugs.*

Morrison's group, The Doors, went on to achieve an almost cult following, and two of its songs, "Break on Through (to the Other Side)" and "When the Music's Over" reflected the psychedelic origin of the band's name. Morrison died in Paris in 1971. Although he was rumored to have succumbed to a drug overdose, his death certificate said "heart attack."

Janis Joplin, who like Jim Morrison was a cultural icon for the generation that came of age in the 1960s, appeared to be using drugs to fight the pain and alienation she grew up with in Port Arthur, Texas, in the 1950s. She did not fit into the society of her oil executive father, and she found no one to share her feelings with. During her years as a star, she became addicted to alcohol and heroin. Joplin died of a heroin overdose in a Los Angeles motel room on October 4, 1970.

Jimi Hendrix, whose astounding feats on electric guitar both exemplified acid rock and heralded the beginning of heavy metal, blasted to the top of the rock scene in the late 1960s. He died in his sleep the same year Joplin overdosed. According to the official record, death was due to "inhalation of vomit following barbiturate intoxication."

The exploits of the Rolling Stones — one of the most successful bands to come out of the 1960s — included drug busts in 1967 that nearly landed lead singer Mick Jagger and lead guitarist Keith Richards in jail. Jagger was arrested in England for possession of pep pills at a party, and Richards was arrested for permitting his house to be used for smoking marijuana. Jagger obtained the drugs legally in Italy and received his own physician's approval of their use once he returned to England. The physician did not, however, give Jagger a written prescription. Reasoning that it was technically illegal for Jagger to have brought in the drugs from abroad without having a doctor prescribe them, the court sentenced him to several months in jail.

In an editorial at the time, the *Times* of London suggested that Jagger was given a jail sentence on this technicality because he was a symbol of decadence and of youthful customs resented by adults. The editorial pointed out that most first offenders are put on probation. The Court of Appeal later quashed the prison sentences of both musicians.

In 1970 Marianne Faithfull, a former girlfriend of Mick Jagger and a recording artist in her own right, entered a hospital to cure her heroin addiction.

In 1969, Jagger was arrested again, this time with his girl friend, singer Marianne Faithfull, for possession of marijuana. Faithfull, the daughter of a London University lecturer on Renaissance studies and an Austrian baroness, had several hit records in the mid-1960s. When she was 18 she released her hit record "As Tears Go By," which was written for her by Jagger and Richards. That year she married a London art dealer, whom she divorced in 1970. By then she had already become Jagger's girl friend and miscarried their baby.

Faithfull later became a heroin addict and was hospitalized after suffering a drug overdose on the movie set of *Ned Kelly*, in which she was to costar with Jagger. She helped write the lyrics for the Rolling Stones' song "Sister Morphine" and appeared in a few movies over the next several years. Following her breakup with Jagger in 1970 she entered a hospital to cure her heroin addiction.

A few years later, Faithfull was back in the recording studio, where she cut three well-received albums during the 1970s.

In 1974 Keith Richards lost an appeal on drug charges in France, was fined, was given a suspended sentence, and was banned from that country for two years. He also was convicted of cocaine possession in England in 1977 and faced a judge in Toronto, Canada, that year for possession of heroin (a cocaine possession charge was dropped for lack of evidence). The prosecuting attorney in the Canadian case said that Richards had been addicted to heroin since 1972. The defense lawyer pointed out that he had been receiving treatment for addiction at the Stevens Psychiatric Center in New York City and was in the process of overcoming a lack of self-confidence and problems with personal relationships.

Richards pleaded guilty to heroin possession but was given a suspended sentence on the condition that he give a benefit concert for the Canadian Institute for the Blind. On April 22, 1979, he gave the concert, which included a guest appearance by Mick Jagger.

Mick Jagger and Keith Richards leave a London court after being charged with drug possession. Earlier in their careers both musicians were apprehended more than once for possession of illegal substances.

The Beatles also became entries on police blotters around the world for their drug arrests. On March 12, 1967, the day Paul McCartney married Linda Eastman in England, Scotland Yard detectives raided the home of George Harrison and arrested him and his wife, Patti, on charges of possessing marijuana.

In 1973 McCartney pleaded guilty to growing five marijuana plants on his farm in western Scotland and paid a fine. Seven years later he was arrested at Japan's New Tokyo International Airport and led away in handcuffs on charges of smuggling into the country about eight ounces of marijuana stashed in his suitcase. He had arrived with his family and members of his singing group, Wings, for an 11-concert tour of Japan. Instead, he spent 10 days in custody and was then deported. The concert tour was canceled.

The Beatles, the most successful rock group of all time, denied that their songs encouraged drug use, but arrests on drug charges multiplied along with their hits during the 1960s and early 1970s.

Fellow Beatle John Lennon's 1968 marijuana conviction in England haunted him years later when he faced deportation from the United States. The U.S. government contended that the arrest in England made him ineligible to become a permanent citizen. His four-year court battle ended in 1976. In October of that year, the U.S. Court of Appeals ruled that the marijuana conviction was not sufficient ground for deportation. In July 1976, a special immigration judge ruled that Lennon's application for permission to remain in the U.S. was formally approved.

Even as drug arrests and deaths mounted during the 1970s, a particularly nihilistic form of rock, punk rock, was beginning to leave its mark. Among its early artists were Patti Smith, the Ramones, and the Sex Pistols. This last group was a particularly violent, abusive band whose members sometimes wore dirty clothes, Nazi regalia, and torn T-shirts in performance. In 1979 Sid Vicious, bass player for the group, died of a heroin overdose in New York while awaiting trial for the murder of his girl friend, Nancy, who was also an addict. The 1986 movie *Sid and Nancy* took a cold, hard look at the doomed couple and graphically portrayed their drug habits.

Heroin, in fact, has been a major drug of abuse among a broad spectrum of rock stars. According to *The Book of Rock Lists* by Dave Marsh and Kevin Stein, former heroin users also include Tim Buckley, Ray Charles, Eric Clapton, James Taylor, Johnny Thunders (of the New York Dolls and the Heartbreakers), and Johnny Winter.

Gregg Allman, of the Allman Brothers Band, became addicted to heroin, and according to *People* magazine, described his addiction as "a cat in my body. His air is used up, and his claws are out."

In 1976 Allman's former road manager, John C. Herring, who allegedly kept the musician supplied with cocaine, was convicted on federal narcotics charges. The conviction came after two days of testimony given by Allman in exchange for a government promise that he himself would not be prosecuted in the case. The U.S. Court of Appeals in New Orleans reversed Herring's conviction in 1978, stating that the newspaper accounts of the matter, including Allman's testimony, could have prejudiced the jury.

John Phillips, the leader of the folk-rock group the Mamas and the Papas, abused drugs throughout the 1960s, at the same time his group rose to fame. By 1975 he was a heroin addict. In August 1980, federal drug agents arrested him at his Long Island home on charges of taking part in a conspiracy to obtain and market tens of thousands of depressant and stimulant drug tablets.

Following his arrest, he and his daughter MacKenzie, a star of the television program "One Day at a Time," who was treated for cocaine addiction (see Chapter 4), entered a drug-treatment program at Fair Oaks Hospital, in Summit, New Jersey.

David Crosby, who left The Byrds to form Crosby, Stills, Nash and Young, ultimately became another cocaine addict. His friends urged him to check into a rehabilitation hospital in 1981, but their efforts were futile. Crosby's long-time collaborator, Graham Nash, even wrote a plea to the addicted artist in the form of a song called "Into the Darkness," which appeared on the group's 1982 album, *Daylight Again*:

A cocaine addict for many years, rock star David Crosby (center, with fellow band members Graham Nash and Stephen Stills) was jailed on drug-possession charges before overcoming the habit in 1987.

Into the darkness soon you'll be sinking.
What are you doing? What can you be thinking?
All of your friends have been trying to warn you.
That some of your demons are dying to drag you
    away into the darkness. *

But in April of that year Crosby was arrested in the dressing room of a Dallas, Texas, nightclub for possession of cocaine, which he was using at the time, and a loaded .45 caliber automatic pistol. He served several months of a five-year prison term before being released on parole in August 1986.

The same year, Belinda Carlisle of the popular all-female group the Go-Gos was making it on her own, without her old group, and without drugs, which she had given up the year before.

"I was drinking a lot, and probably taking too many drugs," she said in a *Rolling Stone* interview. "It wasn't fun anymore. It wasn't working. I wasn't escaping anymore."

Carlisle was supported in her desire to overcome her drug problem by fellow band member Charlotte Caffey, who also had trouble with substance abuse, and had gone through a phase in which she was performing and even giving interviews under the influence of drugs.

"My life was at a very scary point," Caffey told *Rolling Stone*. "I was very out of control as far as drinking and drugs [were concerned], and I knew I had to do something, because I was going to die."

Caffey's decision to check into a drug-rehabilitation center encouraged Carlisle to change her own ways. In fact, Carlisle traces her personal renaissance to March 4, 1985, which was, according to *Rolling Stone*, "The day that she knew it was time to stop acting like a spoiled rock star, time to stop buying the lie that it's natural for rock and rollers to be wild and self-indulgent."

She stopped taking drugs, received help from Alcoholics Anonymous, started a healthy diet, and cut a successful solo album, *Belinda*.

Perhaps the biggest drug story of 1986 involving a singer was Scotland Yard's arrest of rock star George O'Dowd, better known as Boy George, the lead singer of the group Culture

* CREDIT: WRITTEN BY GRAHAM NASH, © 1982 PUTZY, PUTZY MUSIC. USED BY PERMISSION. ALL RIGHTS RESERVED.

British singer Boy George's sudden celebrity during the early 1980s was fleeting. It is said that anguish over his fall from public favor drove him to heroin abuse and addiction.

Club. The police also arrested his brother, Kevin, and several others charged with possession of heroin or conspiring to sell it to the singer.

Boy George burst onto the world rock scene in 1982, complete with heavy makeup and women's clothes — a throwback, in some ways, to the outlandish outfits of Little Richard. Boy George became an international celebrity, a role he undoubtedly cherished.

But in 1984, with success seeming to slip away as his group's ratings plummeted on the charts, Boy George, overcome by worry and uncertainty, began to use heroin. Although he at first denied his problem, he told reporters in July 1986, "You don't have to be a doctor to look at me and know I am dying. I am an out-and-out heroin junkie with an eight-gram-a-day habit."

Boy George underwent a controversial medical treatment that entailed receiving small electrical currents in his brain to stimulate the release of natural brain opiate chemicals called endorphins — the same technique used to treat rock stars Peter Townsend and Eric Clapton for the same problem years earlier.

There is no doubt that musicians have often paid a price for their fame and fortune by succumbing to drugs. Their "fast track" lives, replete with money, travel, easy sex, sycophantic hangers-on, and the greedy adoration of their fans, often promote the kind of instability that can make someone vulnerable to drug abuse. In addition, these idols can easily begin to believe they are invulnerable to the dangers posed by drugs and alcohol. But despite the cases of substance abuse that continue to plague the music industry, it is important to remember that the drug problems within this field are still only part of a much larger drug scene — one that includes business executives, medical professionals, and other more conventional members of society.

The ultimate sex symbol for an entire generation, Marilyn Monroe never found happiness in her success; she craved recognition as a serious actress. She died of a drug overdose at the age of 36.

CHAPTER 3

DRUGS, THE THEATER, AND THE MOVIES

The New York City theater crowd was abuzz with excitement in the fall of 1810. The great British actor George Frederick Cooke, of the Covent Garden Theatre in London, was coming to tour the eastern United States. Officials at the Park Theater in New York had to turn away eager fans from Cooke's premiere performance in Shakespeare's *Richard III*. The critics, for the most part, rejoiced at Cooke's performance, one writer calling it "the product of genius."

On the third night of the show, however, Cooke's voice was hoarse and weak. Most people in the audience assumed he was ill, and applauded him for performing as well as he did. But others knew the real reason Cooke had trouble performing that night: he was intoxicated.

Several weeks after his hoarse performance in New York, Cooke appeared in a play that was unfamiliar to him. This time, intoxicated and unsure, his performance was a fiasco. For the next two years Cooke traveled through the United States performing at leading theaters, sometimes brilliantly, other times unsteadied by drink. A physical wreck at the age of 57, he died in New York in 1812.

Thirty-five years later Edwin Booth, the 13-year-old son of the Shakespearean actor Junius Booth, became his father's traveling companion. Together they traveled the grinding U.S.

Edwin Booth, seen here as Hamlet, was a well-known 19th-century Shakespearian actor. On more than one occasion, Booth disgraced himself by appearing on stage in a state of obvious intoxication.

theater circuit by coach, rail, and river steamer. Not an actor yet, Edwin's job was to coax his father away from alcohol or, failing that, to fetch him from the fire-lit taverns and dirty gutters into which Junius drunkenly stumbled after his rousing performances on stage.

In *Prince of Players*, her biography of Edwin Booth, Eleanor Ruggles recounts a story the actor told years later of his father's desperate, wily efforts to get a drink. Locked in his hotel room from the outside, Junius Booth supposedly bribed a bellboy who was passing by to bring him mint juleps, which he then drank with a straw through the keyhole.

Through his experiences with his father, Edwin developed a passion for the theater and more than a nodding acquaintance with alcohol. On September 10, 1849, Edwin appeared with his father in *Richard III* at the old Boston Museum. It was the beginning of a series of joint appearances.

By late 1852, however, Junius was dead and Edwin was an actor in his own right.

Even before he was out of his teens, Edwin, too, had begun to drink heavily. Within a few years, the younger Booth's drinking had led to his dismissal from the Forrest, a theater in Sacramento, California. On another occasion, after he appeared locally in a play called *The Corsican Brothers*, the *Democratic State Journal* reported, "Mr. Booth, who was cast to sustain the principal character, could hardly sustain himself, but he struggled through it, dragging everything down to the depths of disgust. Speaking mildly, he was intoxicated."

But his sober performances carried his career, and his great talent brought him fame and success.

Booth curtailed his drinking following his marriage to the actress Mary Devlin. But his increasing fame brought him into the limelight more often. Over sumptuous dinners amid friends and admirers, he would drink a glass of wine, which became two glasses, then three . . .

The old days of heavy drinking returned and alcohol again took its toll on his professional reputation. During his 1863 appearance at New York's Winter Garden in *Richard III*, the *Herald's* theater critic wrote, "Seldom have we seen Shakespeare so murdered as at the Winter Garden during the past two weeks. It would have been better to disappoint the public by closing the theater than to place Mr. Booth upon the stage when he was really unfit to act."

At that time his wife was living in Dorchester, Massachusetts, ill and bed-ridden. When her condition worsened, the doctor sent a telegram to Booth at the Winter Garden. There was no answer. At one point, three telegrams lay unopened in Booth's dressing room, where the actor sat, drunk, waiting for his cue to go on.

Finally, his wife's doctor sent a telegram to the manager of the theater, who alerted Booth to his wife's condition. The following morning Booth and a friend left by train for Boston. They were met at the station with the news of Mary's death.

Booth's grief over his loss was intensified by the knowledge that Mary had learned of his sordid behavior in New York. He was convinced that if she had not heard such news about him, she could have rallied from her illness. He vowed to give up drinking.

Booth's resolve was strong and remained so even after he was overwhelmed by the crime committed by his younger brother John Wilkes Booth: the assassination of President Abraham Lincoln.

The legacy of alcohol in the theater has certainly not been limited to the Booth family, nor was it confined to the 19th century. Indeed, some of the finest stage actors of the 20th century have been victims of alcoholism. Some have recovered, some have succumbed.

One of these theatrical greats is the American actor Jason Robards, Jr. Robards was born in Chicago on July 26, 1922, while his father, Jason Robards, Sr., was appearing in a local theater. The family was poor and from 1931 on "there wasn't a dime in our household — we were changing clothes with each other and trying to keep clean and get to school," the younger Robards said in an interview in *Esquire* magazine many years later.

After several unsuccessful attempts, actor Jason Robards, Jr., was finally able to overcome a serious drinking problem when he admitted to himself that alcohol was destroying his talent.

The budding actor, who was struggling to survive in New York after World War II, got his big break when he was chosen to play the lead in Eugene O'Neill's classic play *The Iceman Cometh*. He was a hit, and other roles, in both O'Neill plays and works by Shakespeare, followed. His star rising, he appeared in the film *A Thousand Clowns*, and on television in Ernest Hemingway's *For Whom the Bell Tolls*. His first marriage dissolved, and he remarried.

During this time his reputation as a fine actor sometimes seemed to compete with his image as one of the "legendary boozers of New York." "It's an occupational disease," Robards said in the *Esquire* article. "It goes back to Dionysus and the Greeks." He said it was common among "all of us in the theater who wanted to forget our night's work and pain and family and whatever."

His excessive drinking continued. His second marriage failed, as did his third, to the actress Lauren Bacall. Following the divorce, he married a film production executive. But his acting career was in a downward spiral; he appeared in one undistinguished film after another, including a horror film, *Murders in the Rue Morgue*.

And he kept on drinking.

Then one night in December 1972, he was driving home to his house in Malibu, California, from a night of drinking at a bar, when he crashed his car and was rushed to a hospital.

That night, plastic surgeons and oral surgeons labored to repair his torn upper lip, smashed nose, crushed cheekbones, split palate, and damaged eye socket. The actor's front teeth were literally pushed down his throat, and had to be replaced. In a particularly grisly moment of this catastrophe, Robards began to choke on his own vomit, and additional surgery was required to save his life. During the weeks he spent in the hospital recovering, he also suffered a severe case of pneumonia.

After he left the hospital, the actor promised himself two things. The first of the vows was that he would never again take an acting role in a bad play or movie. A year later, he received rave reviews for his performance in New York in O'Neill's *A Moon for the Misbegotten*.

His second resolution was to stop drinking. But staying dry was much harder than finding good roles; there were times when he went back to the bottle and had to suffer through another withdrawal period.

One night he panicked during a stage performance while suffering from the effects of the previous night's drinking. There was talk of putting the understudy on to replace Robards for the rest of the performance. That was too much for his professional pride.

"*That was it*," Robards recalled. "From that day on, I never took another drink. It took a jolt like that."

Robards continued his newly revived career, and in 1976 and 1977 won consecutive Oscars for his supporting roles in the films *All the President's Men* and *Julia*.

Another formidable presence on stage, Richard Burton (born Richard Jenkins), also drank heavily for many years. He first took to alcohol during his youth in Wales during the 1940s. As a rising star he continued to drink heavily, but it did not seem to affect his work, such as his acclaimed performance as King Arthur in the 1960 Broadway musical *Camelot* for which he won a Tony award. Indeed, four years later, his interpretation of *Hamlet* established him unquestionably as one of the world's great actors.

But his reputation as a great drinker was by now also growing. "From 1968 to 1972," he told a reporter for the *New York Times*, "I was pretty hopeless. I was fairly sloshed for five years."

In mid-April 1974, just after filming *The Klansman* with Lee Marvin, Burton entered St. John's Hospital in Santa Monica, California. By this time, he recounted later, he was drinking up to three bottles a day of hard liquor. After five weeks he left the hospital and dropped out of sight in order to continue his "recuperation." He did not stop drinking, but he did drink less.

In *Richard Burton*, a biography of the actor written by Paul Ferris, the author recounted Burton's admission of his alcoholism during a 1977 television interview. "I think I'm an alcoholic actually, but I'm not entirely sure. Nobody's actually defined what an alcoholic is. But from all the various things I've read about alcoholism, I think I qualify."

Seven years later he was dead, probably of complications arising from his abuse of alcohol.

Recognized as one of the great acting talents of the 20th century, Richard Burton fought a losing battle with alcoholism for most of his life. In 1984 he died of complications caused by this disease.

A year before Burton died, James Hayden, another bright young star on Broadway, was also struggling with a drug habit. Hayden was a heroin addict and at the time was appearing in the role of Bobby, also a heroin addict, in the play *American Buffalo*.

The previous year Hayden had married a woman he met in California. His wife tried unsuccessfully to persuade him to kick his habit, and within months their marriage fell apart. His former wife went back to California but kept in touch with Hayden by phone. During one late-night phone conversation, Hayden simply stopped talking. Concerned, his former wife called the New York police, who forced their way into his apartment and found him slumped over the kitchen sink, dead. Nearby were a hypodermic needle and other drug paraphernalia.

Like the stage, the glittering world of Hollywood celebrity and wealth has nurtured its own crop of drug abusers and drug tragedies. The harvest began early in the history of film: Silent-movie actress Mabel Normand became hooked on narcotics to hide from the pain of finding her best friend in the arms of her boyfriend, moviemaker Mack Sennett.

During those same early days, Wallace Reid, one of the industry's "hot properties" at the time, became hooked on morphine. Reid's habit started after he seriously injured himself while working on a film. The movie company arranged for a physician to administer morphine to kill his pain. When, after repeated doses, Reid became addicted, the movie company made sure the actor had a steady supply of the pain-killing opiates so he could continue to grind out profitable films. On January 18, 1923 Reid died of a morphine overdose while working on the set of a movie.

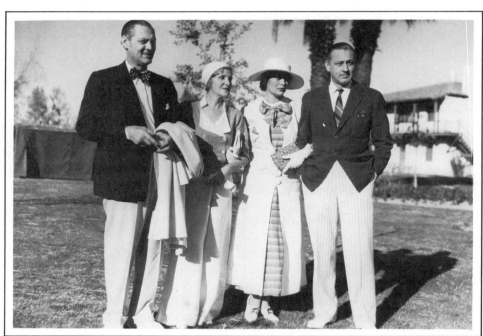

Actors Lionel and John Barrymore pose with their wives. Both brothers had drug-related problems; Lionel became hooked on morphine, which he began taking to ease the pain of his arthritis, and John's drinking exploits were notorious in Hollywood.

Silent-movie actress Mabel Normand, who suffered from narcotics addiction, starred in the Hal Roach comedy Raggedy Rose. Early film stars were idolized celebrities in their time, as vulnerable to drug abuse as are their counterparts of the 1980s.

His distraught wife, Dorothy Davenport, launched an antidrug campaign that included making a film about the dangers of narcotics. This film, *Human Wreckage*, starred Bessie Smith as an addict; it was produced in cooperation with the Los Angeles Anti-Narcotic League, and Will H. Hays, the head of the Motion Picture Producers and Distributors Association. Hays, an aggressive moralist prominent in the film industry at that time, firmly believed in using movies to promote virtue.

The great actor Lionel Barrymore also used narcotics to ease the pain of the severe, crippling arthritis that confined him to a wheelchair in his later years. Newspaper columnist James Bacon recounted in one of his stories how Barrymore confessed to him that MGM studio boss Louis B. Mayer provided him with $500 worth of morphine each day.

"I don't know how or where he gets it," Bacon quoted the actor as saying, "but if he didn't, I would have put a gun to my head years ago."

Although Lionel Barrymore's drug habit might not have been commonly known, his brother John was notorious in Hollywood for his heavy drinking.

A few hours after John Barrymore's death, several of his friends, drunk at the time, stole the dead actor's body from the funeral home. They brought the body to the house of fellow actor Errol Flynn. There, they set the body up in a chair, as if Barrymore were alive. When Flynn later entered the room, he screamed and fled.

As outrageous as that incident was, it was not as unconventional an experience for Flynn as it would probably be for most people. If any screen idol can be said to have led an outrageous life, that person was Errol Flynn.

Born in Hobart, Tasmania, in 1909, Flynn was expelled from school at 16 for nearly killing another boy in a fight. The next year he set out to make his way through the Southwest Pacific, leaving behind his biologist father and a mother, who, years later, referred to him as "a nasty little boy."

Among his exploits were gold prospecting (unsuccessfully) in New Guinea, managing a plantation, and running freight and passengers (including indentured laborers — virtual slaves) along the coast of New Guinea in his own schooner.

Along the way, he was building a reputation for drinking, womanizing, and fighting.

After appearing in a documentary movie, he moved to England, and appeared in a series of commercial films. From there he hopped to the United States, where his films, including *Captain Blood*, *The Charge of the Light Brigade*, and *They Died with Their Boots On*, established his public image as a swashbuckling movie star during the 1930s and 1940s.

But beneath his dashing smile and adventurous, carefree image, he was a troubled figure, searching for a sense of his own identity and struggling to make sense of his life. Along the way he was married three times and fought accusations of statutory rape. And he consumed massive amounts of liquor to help him get by — sometimes two or more quarts in a day. He compounded his problems by using morphine to self-medicate his punishing hangovers. His film career slipped, and his performances became mere shadows of his former triumphs.

In his autobiography, *My Wicked, Wicked Ways*, he wrote, "I crave the indulgence of my senses but this is countered by an interior desire that is even keener than my senses to know the meaning of things."

But indulgence of his senses seemed to have won out anyway.

By the early 1950s he was spending much of his time partying in the international haunts of the rich and famous. While staying at the apartment of a physician in Vancouver, British Columbia, in 1959, enjoying the company of his 17-year-old female companion, he suddenly became ill. He was suffering pains characteristic of a heart attack, with which he was already familiar. Flynn got up from where he was sitting and announced to his companions in the room, "I shall return."

But the 50-year-old former star and long-time drug abuser never did. The doctor who performed the autopsy later said that Flynn had the internal organs of an 80-year-old man.

A few years before Flynn died, another idol of the silver screen suffering from a variety of emotional and psychological woes entered an experimental psychotherapy program. The

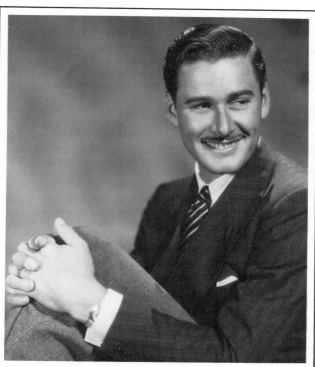

Errol Flynn seemed determined to live a life as colorful as those of the swashbuckling heroes he portrayed so unforgettably on the screen. Abuse of alcohol and morphine contributed to his early death.

man was Cary Grant, whose debonair on-screen persona was the antithesis of the troubled man behind the mask. Grant's psychiatrists, as part of his treatment, administered the hallucinogenic drug lysergic acid diethylamide (LSD) to their famous patient.

Grant attended more than 60 Saturday sessions over 18 months, taking LSD each time.

In his book *Haunted Idol: The Story of the Real Cary Grant*, biographer Geoffrey Wansell quoted the actor as saying of these sessions, "I passed through changing seas of horrifying and happy thoughts, through a montage of intense love and hate, a mosaic of past impressions assembling and reassembling, through terrifying depths of dark despair replaced by heaven-like religious symbolism."

Through this professionally controlled drug administration and supervision — rather than promiscuous abuse — Grant derived substantial benefits, felt better about himself, and, for a while, was an enthusiastic advocate of such therapy.

Grant's use of LSD became a major issue during his divorce from actress Dyan Cannon (the fourth of his five wives) in 1968, during which she testified in court that during their marriage he had had screaming fits caused by LSD "trips" and sometimes became violent. She wanted to restrict Grant's access to their daughter. But two psychiatrists who had examined Grant testified that he appeared to have suffered no damage and did not constitute a threat to his daughter. In the end, the judge ruled that the previous episodes of violence could have been due to LSD, but that since Grant was no longer using the drug, the violence "may no longer be a problem." He also stated that the actor appeared to be "a loving and devoted father" who should be entitled to visiting rights.

Not only did Cary Grant get visiting rights, but the next year his lawyers arranged for a substantial increase in those rights.

While Grant was enjoying some of his earliest film successes during the late 1930s, a gifted young performer was beginning her career at MGM, the studio that produced some of the greatest movie musicals of the era. That performer was Judy Garland, who delighted millions as Dorothy in the classic

Cary Grant in Alfred Hitchcock's 1957 suspense thriller North by Northwest. *The actor took LSD regularly as part of psychiatric treatment he underwent during the 1950s.*

movie *The Wizard of Oz* but whose life behind the scenes was a morass of pressures and worries exacerbated by a lack of family support and an excess of drugs.

Her father died when she was 12, and Garland was raised by her mother, whom she later described as "the real-life Wicked Witch of the West." With no home life to speak of, she became a child of the MGM movie studio. The studio was demanding and the hours sometimes very long. Her introduction to drugs came early and without her knowledge.

Studio boss Louis B. Mayer, eager to keep his young star "up" so she could perform, as well as stay thin, arranged to have her given amphetamines to pep her up and barbiturates to put her to sleep when she was not needed on the set.

Her fifth husband, Mickey Deans, recalled his wife's drug diet in his biography of her, *Weep No More My Lady*, which he co-wrote with Ann Pinchot.

"We were working six days a week, ten to twelve hours a day," he quoted his wife as telling him. "I had plenty of vitality and endurance, but this was a grind. When I began

Mickey Rooney and Judy Garland in a scene from the 1939 film Babes in Arms. *Said Garland of the way she was treated as a child actress: "The monkey Cheetah was treated better than I was. At least Cheetah got a banana to eat . . . all I got was a barbiturate."*

to sag, the studio doctor fed me and some of the other young performers pills that looked as big as plates. They were supposed to keep us peppy. They sure did. We were wound up like waltzing mice. When I finished shooting, they'd take me over to the studio hospital, where they had a little bed for me. The monkey Cheetah was treated better than I was. At least Cheetah got a banana to eat. All I got was a barbitruate popped in my mouth — until four hours later, when they'd wake me up and put a pep pill in my mouth so I could go back to the sound stage and work another long stretch."

The pattern continued into her adulthood. By the time Deans had met Garland, he wrote, the singer habitually carried a bottle of Ritalin, an antidepressant, in her pocketbook.

"The prospect of running out of pills made her hysterical," according to Deans's account.

"Fortified by them, she could face the showbiz pressures, the promotions, the incessant demands, as well as the strain of the performance itself, the fear that she might have lost the touch, that her voice was betraying her, that the magical communication between her and the audience had been broken."

Her career was at first a resounding success; among her most popular films were *Meet Me in St. Louis*, *Easter Parade*, and *A Star Is Born*. Her singing concerts were triumphs. But by age 47, she was on her fifth marriage, had been on numerous alcohol and pill binges, and had struggled back from physical and professional oblivion several times.

In July 1969, just at a time when she was planning a comeback, Garland died from an accidental overdose of barbiturates.

Another actress haunted by the specter of drugs throughout her life was the hearthrob of millions of men during the 1950s and remains a subject of fascination decades after her death. The actress, born Norma Jean Baker, was raised in an orphanage and married at age 14. She later changed her name to Marilyn Monroe and took Hollywood by storm in such movies as *All About Eve*, *The Seven Year Itch*, *Bus Stop*, and the classic comedy *Some Like It Hot*.

Much has been written about the tormented life of Marilyn Monroe — her search for recognition as a serious actress, her broken marriages to baseball great Joe DiMaggio and playwright Arthur Miller. She was a superstar during the 1950s, but she became a Hollywood legend the hard way. Although conspiracy theories have attracted considerable attention, her death in 1962 at the age of 36 is generally attributed to suicide by an overdose of sedatives.

As movie audiences were still pondering Monroe's tragic death during the early 1960s, another movie actress, Mercedes McCambridge, who won an Oscar in 1949 as supporting actress in her first film role, in *All the King's Men*, was caught in the quagmire of alcoholism.

Ironically, it was McCambridge's decision to go public with her problem after she recovered that seemed to damage her career. She had agreed to testify at a U.S. Senate hearing

into the disease of alcoholism in order to help publicize this major public health problem, to encourage other alcoholics to seek treatment, and to urge officials to ensure that money was available to treat them.

"Nobody need die of this disease," she told the senators as news cameras whirred in the hearing room. "We are well worth the trouble. We are eminently equipped to enrich this world. We write poetry, we paint pictures, we compose music, we build bridges, we head corporations, we win the coveted prizes for the world's greatest literature, and too often too many of us die from our disease, not our sin, not our weakness."

Whatever effect her testimony had on raising the consciousness of people, her appearance at least raised the hackles of some of those people who hire actors.

"I can say that demand for my acting services fell off sharply," McCambridge wrote in her autobiography, *The Quality of Mercy*, "following my testimony in July 1969 before the Senate Subcommittee on Alcoholism and Narcotics."

McCambridge's book contains a harrowing description of her effort to cure herself of the "shakes" she suffered early one Sunday morning after a party the night before that included heavy drinking in the apartment she had sublet in New York.

The wrung-out actress dragged herself into her little kitchen, and at almost six o'clock in the morning, with no booze in the apartment, was searching desperately for anything that had alcohol in it. She found a bottle of wine vinegar in the refrigerator and took a drink.

"The immediate insult to my system," she wrote, "forced out a violent stream of bile that threw my head back as it shot from my mouth. I lay down on the floor, on my back, gasping. I was going into hysterics. I was naked and foul-smelling from the rancid spittle in my hair and on my chest. 'Oh my God, I'm sorry! Oh, great good God, I'm so sorry! *Is this me?* Oh, God, God, God, is this really me?' And of course it was. It was me."

Having hit rock bottom with alcohol, McCambridge was able to go on and conquer her addiction. Actor William Holden (born William Franklin Beedle) was not so lucky. Holden,

One of Hollywood's most popular actors, William Holden had a serious drinking problem for most of his career. His accidental death after a drinking binge is one of Hollywood's saddest losses to drug abuse.

the "golden boy" of Hollywood, played leading roles in *Golden Boy*, *The Bridge on the River Kwai*, *Paris When It Sizzles*, and *Network*. In private life he was as much of an adventurer as some of the characters he played on film. He loved Africa, particularly the dangers lurking in the wilds of Kenya. There he worked and invested money in efforts to save endangered animal species.

"Every day in Africa might be your last," he once said to a friend. "That sense of anticipation keeps you thrillingly alive!" Ironically, Holden was slowly killing himself with alcohol.

Writer Bob Thomas, who knew the actor for 35 years, wrote in *Golden Boy: The Untold Story of William Holden* that alcohol was Holden's way of easing the pain of guilt: guilt that his younger brother Robert died in combat during World War II, while he had easy duty in the United States; guilt that his younger brother Richard had to work hard to make a living, while his own success came easily; guilt that he was working in an undignified, "unmanly" profession; guilt that he was a poor father; and guilt that he was "an inconsistent husband."

At first, Holden's drinking did not interfere with his work. Indeed, he won the best-actor Oscar in 1953 for his work in *Stalag 17*.

But during the 1962 filming of *Paris When It Sizzles*, Holden was drinking throughout the day. Sometimes filming was canceled because he could not perform. At one point he entered a hospital for alcoholics for an eight-day treatment, at the end of which he completed filming the movie.

The end came in November 1981, in an apartment in Shoreham Tower, a building in Santa Monica, California, of which he was part owner. The building manager opened the door of the apartment where Holden had been staying, alone, for several days. He found the actor lying in a pool of blood. An empty bottle of vodka in the kitchen wastebasket and a full bottle near the bed indicated how the doomed star had spent his last few days alone.

Dr. Thomas T. Noguchi, the coroner for the County of Los Angeles, theorized that Holden had slipped on a throw rug, hit his head on the sharp corner of the bedside table, and then slumped onto the bed. Although the actor had tried to stop the bleeding with tissues, which were also found near the body, he lost consciousness and died within a half hour after the accident.

"What a lousy fadeout for a great guy," director William Wyler commented to the *New York Times*.

Lee Marvin also earned a reputation as a heavy drinker; he became notorious for his violent rowdiness while under the influence of alcohol. His macho image and love of guns is no Hollywood put-on. Marvin fought with the U.S. Marines in the Pacific islands during World War II, participating in some of the bloodiest battles there against the Japanese. He was wounded during one of those battles, and transferred back to the United States.

After establishing himself as an actor, Marvin earned his tough-guy screen image in films such as *The Wild One*, *The Big Heat*, *The Killers*, and *The Dirty Dozen*. But it was his

Lee Marvin in the film version of Ernest Hemingway's The Killers. *Off the screen, the tough-guy actor sometimes used his gun on the streets after consuming too much alcohol.*

comedic performance as a drunken gunfighter in *Cat Ballou* that won him an Oscar. He also starred in over 100 television episodes as a tough police detective in "M-Squad."

Marvin's heavy drinking started in 1949-50 during his early days in New York trying to break into the big time. During his subsequent highly successful career, his drinking led to memorable destructive incidents.

For example, during the "wrap" party after the completion of a film called *The Losers*, he turned over the 30-foot long hors d'oeuvres table and pinned director Sam Peckinpah against a wall.

Marvin was also known to shoot out streetlights while filming on location, and according to Donald Zec, entertainment columnist for the London *Daily Mirror*, was once stopped in his car by Hollywood police after he drove down a street, dressed in a red, black, and yellow bathrobe, shooting at mail boxes. In his biography of the actor, *Marvin: The Story of Lee Marvin*, Zec recounted how his wife, Betty, despairing over Marvin's drinking, mayhem, and outrageous behavior at parties, finally divorced him.

Although Marvin never gave up drinking completely, his alcohol consumption has trailed off, and the old days are over.

"Anyway," Zec quoted Marvin about his reluctance to resume his heavy drinking, "there comes a time when you've got to ask yourself, 'What for?' "

The connection between drugs and Hollywood has continued into the 1970s and 1980s. Actress Linda Blair, whose portrayal of a girl possessed by the devil chilled many viewers of *The Exorcist*, was arrested in 1979 for cocaine possession, put on three years' parole and fined $5,000.

By 1982, at the age of 26, Melanie Griffith, the beautiful child actress who appeared in *Night Moves* and *The Drowning Pool*, was reassessing her alcohol-, drug-, and sex-filled life. Her career was in need of rejuvenation. She cleaned up her act and starred in *Body Double* and *Something Wild*.

The year after Griffith reassessed her life, Massachusetts state police charged actress Jodie Foster with possession of cocaine at Logan International Airport in Boston. Customs officials stopped her at the airport on December 19, 1983, and discovered that she was carrying a small amount of the

Judy Garland embraces daughter Liza Minnelli after Liza's performance in a 1963 off-Broadway show. Twenty-one years later, Minnelli would admit herself to the Betty Ford Center for treatment of her drug dependency.

drug. The officials reported that Foster admitted the substance was cocaine and paid a $100 fine.

In 1984 Judy Garland's daughter, Liza Minnelli, announced that she had become dependent on alcohol and the tranquilizer Valium and checked into the Betty Ford Center. The center was founded by and named for the wife of former president Gerald R. Ford. Mrs. Ford established the center in 1982 following her own successful treatment for alcoholism and dependency on painkillers and tranquilizers.

The hard-working daughter of film director Vincente Minnelli, Liza drew rave reviews at age 19 for her 1965 performance in the Broadway show *Flora, the Red Menace*, for which she received a Tony award. She went on to win the 1972 Oscar for best actress for her performance in the film *Cabaret*.

But in addition to reveling in success and fame, Minnelli suffered two broken marriages, a string of failed romances, and professional frustrations. Drugs were already part of her

Richard Dreyfuss, who won the Academy Award for best actor in 1977, was charged with drug possession more than once, but stopped using drugs only after a vision warned him of their lethal dangers.

social scene and they became convenient weapons in her personal battle against the "demons" that tormented this talented Broadway and film singer-actress, who, according to friends, could not seem to relax.

After her release from the Betty Ford Center, Minnelli resumed her career. Appropriately enough she sang during her comeback performance a song that urges: "Pick yourself up, dust yourself off, and start all over again."

By the early 1980s, Richard Dreyfuss, who starred in *American Graffiti, Jaws, Close Encounters of the Third Kind*, and *The Goodbye Girl*, had become a heavy user of both alcohol and cocaine. The abuse led to his arrest in October 1982 after he lost control of his car and crashed into a tree. In September 1983 a Beverly Hills, California, judge determined that the actor had made satisfactory progress in a drug counseling program and dismissed two felony drug-possession charges against him.

In an interview published in *Parade* magazine, he said that, following his hospitalization to recover from the crash, he stopped abusing alcohol and drugs. Dreyfuss said he had had a vision. In his mind's eye he saw a young girl wearing a pink-and-white dress, black patent leather shoes, and white socks. Dreyfuss explained that he suddenly realized that she was the little girl he had avoided killing by halting his reckless behavior.

His story is strangely reminiscent of the experience of the 19th-century writer Thomas De Quincey, who used opium. While under the influence of this drug, he witnessed the near-collision of the runaway mail coach he was riding in with a small cart carrying a young man and woman. In his opium stupor, the scene of the young girl standing up, screaming in terror at the onrushing coach, made an indelible impression on him. He wove that vision into the third part of his poem, "The English Mail Coach," in which a runaway coach almost kills a young girl.

The coincidental similarity of the experiences of Dreyfuss and De Quincey exemplifies the commonality of drug-related visions conjured in the artistic mind. But it also stands as a warning of the potentially disastrous consequences of drug abuse, both for the abuser and for those people who suffer directly or indirectly from the abuser's actions.

"Miami Vice" stars Don Johnson and Philip Michael Thomas accepting the People's Choice Award in 1986. This was also the year that Johnson committed himself to give up alcohol and cigarettes.

CHAPTER 4

THE SMALL SCREEN

In 1981, *TV Guide* published an investigative report entitled "Hollywood's Cocaine Connection." The article set off a firestorm of debate between those who claimed that Hollywood did indeed have a major drug problem and those who believed that the problem was being exaggerated.

Even the *TV Guide* article seemed paradoxical. It quoted an anonymous "high-ranking" network official as saying, "Coke is all over the place. It's directors, writers, producers, actors, everyone. It's horrendous." Yet in the next paragraph the story stated, "Obviously, not everyone in the television industry uses cocaine. The users are doubtless a minority."

But the report also stated that offers of drugs were sometimes part of the business deals that determined which programs were put on television. Instead of talent always determining what reached the home viewers, drug bribes sometimes smoothed the way.

Some industry people also complained that technicians, actors, and writers under the influence of drugs caused production delays, gave poor performances, or wrote poor scripts.

Susan Richardson, a star of the series "Eight Is Enough," told a *TV Guide* reporter that performers under the influence of cocaine are "so screwed up" that it requires "30 or 40 or 50 takes" before they get a scene right. "It puts a lot of pressure on the other actors," she said. "How many times can you do a heavy emotional scene?"

The article also quoted Henry Winkler, star of "Happy Days," as saying that working with someone who is on cocaine "gets in your way." Winkler said that although such performers might think they are doing their best work, "they literally are giving you gibberish." Another source said that cocaine users destroy situation comedy series because the drug ruins the performer's sense of timing of jokes and funny situations.

About a year and a half after the *TV Guide* article appeared, the *New York Times* reported that the use of illegal drugs was so widespread in Hollywood that insurance companies had begun to change their policies to avoid having to pay money if drug abuse was the cause of insurance claims. Insurance companies even began to refuse to insure movie productions that featured two or more male stars who had a reputation for drug abuse.

The newspaper reported that in 1981 the Los Angeles County Sheriff's Department had even arrested ten people who were part of a gang that sold cocaine to Hollywood celebrities, making daily deliveries to their homes by limousine.

Another newspaper, the *Los Angeles Herald Examiner*, reported in 1982 that drug abuse by just one individual had ruined a new television comedy show called "Fridays," which was a late night series similar to "Saturday Night Live." The show, which premiered in 1980, was supposed to appeal to young television viewers who would appreciate wild, satirical, and sometimes drug-related humor. The cast was composed of talented young comics, the newspaper reported, and the creative staff was made up of slick, enthusiastic young writers. But the script supervisor was reportedly so handicapped by his addiction to cocaine that he often finished writing the final script just minutes before the cast had to face a live audience, leaving them little time to become familiar with their material. Moreover, the final scripts lacked the wit and imagination that had made "Saturday Night Live" a hit. "Fridays" failed.

The original cast members of the television comedy series "Saturday Night Live." The show's drug-related humor helped make it a hit, but drug abuse among some regulars and guests was not a laughing matter.

But "Saturday Night Live" was not without its own share of problems. For example, while rehearsing for the premiere show of the series in October 1975, the cast found the guest host, comedian George Carlin, distant and difficult to work with, according to the book *Saturday Night: A Backstage History of "Saturday Night Live"* by Doug Nill and Jeff Weingrad. Carlin later admitted he was on cocaine at the time.

Another host of that series, musician Kris Kristofferson, who had a long history of alcohol abuse, drank wine and tequila during the week of rehearsals before the show he was to host. He was reportedly so drunk during dress rehearsal on the day of the show that the cast tried to figure out who should play Kristofferson's parts in the various skits in which he was to appear. Kristofferson was pumped with coffee and did go on, but he barely made it through the show.

The problems of Carlin and Kristofferson, along with those of Saturday Night Live regulars Chevy Chase and John Belushi (see Chapter 5), have been well publicized. They are not, however, the only illustrations of the cost of drug abuse to celebrities in the television industry.

One of these television stars who suffered through a bout with drug abuse is Edd Byrnes, star of the detective series "77 Sunset Strip," who degenerated from a teenage idol of the 1960s to a puffy-faced alcoholic with stomach problems.

According to the journal *Alcoholism and Addiction*, Byrnes's father died from alcoholism when Edd was 13, and the son swore to himself that he would never end up like that. But an ostensible interest in fine wines eventually led to addiction. "First it was wine with lunch," according to Byrnes, "and wine with dinner. Then it was wine with wine, followed by bottles of wine, and I was off and running."

After drinking all day he would get into his car and drive, keeping a lookout in the rearview mirror for the red lights of a police car behind him. He called it a "horrible way to live, always looking over my shoulder." He recalled the panic he felt whenever a police car pulled up behind or next to him in traffic, and he tried to hide his glass of wine.

As is often the case, Byrnes's excessive alcohol consumption caused profound sleep disturbances; to combat his insomnia he began to take sleeping pills, which further undermined his physical and psychological strength. His drinking got worse, and to his daily consumption of wine he added screwdrivers (orange juice and vodka) and champagne mixed with orange juice.

Severe stomach problems drove him to the hospital time and again, and he began to pass blood. In 1982, distraught, disgusted with himself, and urged on by friends, Byrnes finally sought help and overcame his problem.

In addition to his acting career, which has included roles on "Love Boat," "Fantasy Island," and "Simon and Simon," Byrnes now travels the country speaking at treatment centers, dinners, and conferences, sharing his own story and showing a dramatic film on addiction called *I Really Don't Want To Know.* "I have to always remember," he told *Alcoholism and Addiction*, "that I am powerless over alcohol, and that it makes my life unmanageable."

Drug abuse also made MacKenzie Phillips's life unmanageable and led, in January 1978, to charges of disorderly

Singer John Phillips (bottom right) and his daughter MacKenzie, a former cast member of the television series "One Day at a Time," both overcame serious drug problems that threatened their careers. They appeared on "The Dick Cavett Show" in 1981 with Dr. Mark Gold (top left), founder of the cocaine hotline 1-800-COCAINE.

conduct under the influence of drugs or alcohol. Phillips, a star of *One Day at a Time*, was found lying semiconscious on a Hollywood street the previous November; following her arrest, she asked to be sent to a drug treatment facility.

Although authorities said they found traces of alcohol and the sedative Quaalude in her blood the night Phillips lay in the street, the young actress also had a cocaine problem. When she was 17, she flew from Hollywood to London to seek help from her father, John Phillips (see Chapter 2). Instead of help, she found her heroin-addicted father locked in a bathroom. Both ended up in a drug-treatment program.

Another television series, "Mike Hammer," simply stopped production in 1985 while its star, Stacey Keach, served a prison term in England for cocaine possession.

"So distorted was my perspective," Keach later told *Alcoholism and Addiction*, "that I was unwilling, unable to face the truth that the drug had begun to dominate my life. It wasn't until I was apprehended on April 3, 1984, in Heathrow Airport," he continued, "that the shock of recognition finally jolted me into realizing that the drug was controlling me, and that I was helplessly at its mercy."

Actress Heather Thomas of the "Fall Guy" series received help from her family that probably saved her the bother of legal hassles or the specter of serious health problems.

According to a *People* magazine interview, Thomas started abusing drugs in the sixth grade, when she took LSD. After joining the cast of "Fall Guy," she frequently abused the prescription drug Lasix, a diuretic (anti-fluid retention agent) that can cause nervous-system disorders and strokes if not taken under a doctor's supervison. It is *not* meant to be used as a diet aid. Although Thomas lost 20 pounds, she often found it impossible to stay awake during the day — lethargy is a common side effect of this drug when it is abused — so she stimulated herself with cocaine. One day in 1984, she fainted during the filming of the series.

Alarmed when she learned of her daughter's condition, Thomas's mother tricked her into going to St. John's Hospital in Santa Monica, California, by telling her that her father had been admitted there. When the actress arrived at the hospital, however, she was greeted by friends and family members who urged her to check into the hospital's drug detoxification and treatment clinic.

"If my family hadn't intervened," she later told *People*, "I probably would have gone on my merry way until I lost my job or I died."

In addition to those celebrities who have used drugs recreationally, some performers have become addicted to drugs that they had been taking for medical purposes.

Eileen Brennan, who at the time was starring in the series "Private Benjamin," began her addiction while recovering from an accident. A car struck her on the night of October 27, 1982, as she was crossing a street in Venice, California. Brennan lay on the street near death, with both legs crushed, skull and facial bones fractured, and one eye socket shattered. Physicians repaired her body with surgery and eased her terrible pain with the narcotics Demerol, Dilaudid, and morphine.

Eileen Brennan (right) posed with French actress Jeanne Moreau as they began rehearsals for a Broadway play in 1985. Brennan has overcome both alcoholism and drug addiction in the course of her career.

Brennan's body healed, but she became addicted to the drugs. After a failed attempt to cure her addiction through hospitalization — she kicked painkillers but started taking antidepressants — Brennan checked into the Betty Ford Center. The day she checked in, September 1, 1984, actress and singer Liza Minelli was checking out.

"I knew Liza, but I didn't know that she was being discharged the day I checked in," Brennan said in an interview with *Ladies Home Journal.* "She came in to see me, put her arms around me and said, 'It's going to be all right.' All I could do was cry."

The daughter of alcoholic parents, Brennan had had to kick an alcohol habit several years before. Her treatment at the Betty Ford Center in 1984 was her second major victory over drugs.

During her stay at the center Brennan became friendly with another actress undergoing treatment there: Mary Tyler Moore. Moore, a star of "The Dick Van Dyke Show" during

During the 1960s, Mary Tyler Moore and Dick Van Dyke costarred in the hit television series "The Dick Van Dyke Show." Van Dyke went public with his drinking problem years ago. Moore sought help for alcohol dependency in the mid-1980s.

the 1960s and the acclaimed "Mary Tyler Moore Show" in the 1970s, is a diabetic, and has been giving herself injections of insulin for many years. She sometimes engaged in social drinking, especially to relax from the pressures of show business. Unfortunately, the alcohol eventually interfered with Tyler's ability to control her disease. Her husband, a physician, decided it was time to help his wife overcome her habituation to social drinking. Her treatment at the center helped her learn to lead her life without alcohol.

Daniel J. Travanti of the police series "Hill Street Blues" is another television actor who was able to recover from alcoholism. Travanti joined Alcoholics Anonymous soon after he collapsed during a stage performance. Years later, during one episode of "Hill Street Blues," the character he plays on the show attends an Alcoholics Anonymous meeting with one of his subordinates from the precinct, who also has a drinking problem.

Susan St. James, who later was to star in the comedy series "Kate and Allie," began to drink heavily in 1981, while she was living on the West Coast and her husband, Dick Ebersol, was working in New York. "I was flying back and forth, and I started drinking a lot," she told *McCall's* magazine in an interview. "Dick would be working late, and I'd go out drinking with my friends."

She sobered up and quit the bottle after getting drunk one night with her father in a New York bar. Father and daughter pledged that whichever of them was the first to take another drink had to check into an alcoholism clinic.

The use of drugs continues in Hollywood, and some television celebrities no doubt have used drugs for years out of the glare of publicity. The celebrities discussed above represent only some of those stars who have indulged in drugs and suffered the consequences. In the case of Daniel J. Travanti and "Dallas" star Linda Gray, who was able to beat her drinking problem through psychotherapy, those consequences were translated into scripts. Travanti's alcohol problem inspired the scene in which he attended Alcoholics Anonymous. Perhaps drawing on her own experiences, Linda

Daniel J. Travanti speaks at a press conference. Travanti, who played a former alcoholic on the television series "Hill Street Blues," overcame a real-life drinking problem himself.

Gray, as Sue Ellen Ewing of "Dallas" fame, endured the degradation, suffering, and self-doubt of an alcoholic on the skids, undergoing treatment, and fighting to stay off the bottle despite the goading of her husband, J.R. Ewing.

Other television programs, including the soap operas "The Young and the Restless," "All My Children," "Another World," and "As the World Turns," portrayed characters suffering from drug abuse and traced their fates.

A long list of prime-time programs, among them "Fall Guy," "Love Boat," "Happy Days," "Cagney and Lacey," "The Jeffersons," "Simon and Simon," "Knots Landing," "Knight Rider," "Facts of Life," and "The Cosby Show," have also dealt with drugs and drug abuse in at lease one of their episodes.

Another series, "Miami Vice," became a hit that emphasized fashion, music, and its popular stars. Its hard-hitting scripts often dealt with drugs and drug dealing. Don Johnson, who became a star playing the role of an undercover police detective on the series, had many years earlier traveled through the United States working part-time and trying to become an actor. Along the way he indulged heavily in drugs, especially alcohol, marijuana, and cocaine.

The drugs took a greater toll on him than he had bargained for. Trying to recall his New York days for a *Rolling Stone* interview, he said, "The reefer took a toll on my memory." His "drug-addled youth" behind him, Johnson gave up drugs completely in 1986.

In the mid-1980s television began to make an effort to deglamorize drugs and has encouraged education and treatment programs for its own employees. This has not solved the drug abuse problem, of course, since it is really a problem of society as a whole, and not of any one industry or art form. But it *has* certainly enhanced society's awareness of this issue.

Richard Pryor arrives at the premiere of his movie Silver Streak. Pryor's heavily publicized drug problem almost cost him his life.

CHAPTER 5

THE COMEDY CONNECTION

It is around the turn of the century.

Bobbing in the waters off Atlantic City, a young man yells desperately for help. Two able-bodied Samaritans rush into the sea, swim to the drowning man, and pull him to shore. Limp and still, the victim looks dead. So the rescuers carry him into a beer-garden pavilion, place him onto a stage where entertainers ordinarily perform and begin to revive the young man.

A curious, excited crowd gathers to see the high drama played out to the end. Meanwhile, busy waiters do a brisk business selling beer to the onlookers. The limp body shows signs of life. The young man who was snatched from the sea opens his eyes. And the crowd goes wild. The young man is alive. The rescuers are heroes. The curious onlookers get a good show. And the beer garden makes money on the deal.

The deal, in fact, was a phony drowning-and-rescue scenario calculated to attract customers to the beer garden. The two heroes were actors, as was the "victim," a young man named William Claude Dukenfield.

Claude would later change his name to William Claude Fields, and theater and movie audiences would come to love him as W. C. Fields.

The legendary comic actor W. C. Fields, who often played heavy-drinking characters, suffered from the same problem himself, and eventually died from the effects of long-term alcohol abuse.

Born in Philadelphia in 1880, Fields ran away from home when he was 11 years old, after fighting with his father. He lived off the streets and did odd jobs to survive. He lifted himself out of obscurity by learning to juggle, found a job in an act at an amusement park when he was 14, and eventually became a full-fledged entertainer who performed in Broadway theaters.

In 1925 Fields broke into the movies and brought to the screen his famous red, bulbous nose, black cocked hat, and mighty thirst for drink. In films such as *My Little Chickadee* and *Never Give a Sucker an Even Break*, Fields portrayed heavy-drinking characters who had as much love for booze as they had hatred for children.

Of course, the alcohol caught up with him. Fields was forced to spend eight months in a sanitarium in 1936–37 because of complications caused by pneumonia and an over-indulgence in Scotch and sodas.

A few months after recording one of his funniest bits, a "Temperance Lecture," his alcohol-wracked body gave out.

He died on Christmas Day, 1946, leaving in his will $1,535 worth of liquor to his agent, his brother, and a friend.

As jaunty as W. C. Fields was in his movies, comedian Buster Keaton projected an equally memorable image of the dejected, put-upon victim of life's unfairness.

Keaton started his stage career as an infant on the vaudeville stage with his father, Joseph, and his mother, Myra. By the time he was six years old, he had traveled the United States with his parents. As part of the act, Joseph would rough up little Buster on stage. In real life, the father, who was often drunk, regularly beat little Buster.

The beatings took their toll.

As biographer Tom Dardis pointed out in *Keaton*, his biography of the great comedian: "Early photographs reveal a sullen face that glares back at the camera with the expression of someone who has undergone a terrible violation. It is a face that asks to be left alone."

Alcoholism severely damaged the career of Buster Keaton, who symbolized the pathetic and downtrodden outsider in his most famous comic roles.

By the time he was 30 years old, drinking was a major part of Keaton's life, as it had been with his father. A classic alcoholic, he had a large capacity for liquor and regularly denied he had a problem. But his alcoholism became so serious during the 1930s that he would sometimes go on extended drinking binges and disappear for several days or a week.

Both his drinking and his angry artistic arguments with MGM, his employer, contributed to crippling his promising career. He did make memorable films, however, including the now classic *The General*, which was flop in its time. But his first marriage, to Natalie Talmadge, failed, as did his second to practical nurse May Scribbens. Scribbens met Keaton when she was assigned to care for him by the comedian's physician. Around the time they married, Keaton was fired by MGM.

In 1940 Keaton married his third wife, a dancer at MGM named Eleanor Norris who was much younger than he was. Although feeling better about his life after marrying Eleanor, Keaton's drinking continued—sometimes for days on end.

In 1946 the studio laid off Eleanor as well, and Keaton decided to move to Paris to revive his career. Keaton returned to the United States in the 1950s and made several more movies before his death in 1966.

As it did with W. C. Fields, alcohol played a large role in the legend of Jackie Gleason, whose television series "The Honeymooners" has become a classic.

Like Fields, Gleason, who was born in 1916, grew up without a father. His father, like Buster Keaton's father an alcoholic, disappeared shortly before Christmas in 1925, a few days after a violent argument with Gleason's mother.

In his biography of Gleason, *How Sweet It Is*, writer James Bacon (a reporter and longtime friend of the comedian) recounts what might be the beginning of Gleason's awesome drinking style.

The 19-year-old Gleason had just performed a stand-up comedy routine at Tiny's Chateau in Reading, Pennsylvania — his first big break in show business. He bombed, and the owner told him that after his second show that night, he was through. But the owner felt sorry for the young comedian and bought him drinks at the bar in between shows. According to Bacon, "Jackie recalls downing about 15 scotches."

Jackie Gleason, best known for the television series "The Honeymooners," has also gained notoriety for his heavy drinking both on and off the stage.

Drunk, fired, and with nothing to lose, young Gleason walked on stage during his last show and insulted the town of Reading, the tavern owner, and the customers. That and a little singing and dancing composed what he figured would be his final appearance at Tiny's. But the audience loved the show. They laughed and cheered, and the owner held him over for an extra week. Gleason's only problem was that this second show was completely ad-libbed. He did not remember much of it. The next night Gleason got to the tavern early and started to "drink back" his act.

By the 1940s Gleason was a successful comedian, doing his act in theatres and starring in Broadway shows. And he was drinking heavily at Toots Shor's, a famous "watering hole" in Manhattan. In fact, he sometimes had to borrow money to keep up with his bar bill.

The 1950s brought Gleason success in television with "The Honeymooners," but in 1956 his 16-year marriage broke up — a victim, at least in part not only of Gleason's schedule but of his continuous drinking as well.

In 1959 Gleason appeared on Broadway in *Take Me Along*, the musical-comedy version of playwright Eugene O'-Neill's play *Ah, Wilderness*. Gleason played the role of a heavy drinker in the show and won a Tony award for his performance. Among his other fine performances on stage and in the movies, Gleason also portrayed the eccentric, heavy-drinking father of a silent movie star in the movie *Papa's Delicate Condition*. During the filming of that movie, Gleason's dressing room was a mockup of Toots Shor's bar. The joke was apt. Even on live television, "The Great One," as he came to be known, sometimes drank 100-proof "coffee."

The personal and public images of Jackie Gleason have merged in some ways. The heavy drinker portrayed on stage, screen, and television reflects the private person off stage, sitting in a bar, buying the next round for himself and his friends.

Another comedian who enjoyed stardom during the 1950s was Sid Caesar, whose Saturday night programs, "Your Show of Shows" and "Caesar's Hour," were immensely popular. But he was haunted by his troubled youth and by his fear of success.

Caesar's father, a luncheonette owner in Yonkers, New York, was destroyed financially by the Depression. Young Sid, who was only seven or eight years old at the time, wrote that he was devastated to see his father "crumble before my eyes."

Much later, when he was a star, it seemed to Sid Caesar that success had happened too quickly and easily. He felt guilty and afraid. He feared that his talent, which was the source of his wealth and fame, might be just a fleeting gift that would disappear one day right in the middle of a performance. He even feared the autonomy he had in running his own television shows — there was no one to guide him or constrain him.

Caesar attempted to escape his fears, insecurities, and guilt with alcohol. His heavy drinking after work worried the network, NBC, which arranged for him to receive medical treatment. Yet as part of that treatment, he was given another drug, a barbiturate called Tuinal, to which he also became addicted. Caesar's dual addiction caught up with him in 1978.

From January to April of that year he stayed at home, usually in bed. At one point he was consuming eight Tuinals and a quart of scotch a day.

That summer he got out of the house and traveled to Canada to star in the show *Last of the Red Hot Lovers*. But he could not remember his lines. He could not remember where to stand on stage. And he could no longer avoid dealing with his drug abuse problem.

Caesar checked into a hospital and went through the agony of barbiturate withdrawal. Several years afterward, drug-free and rejuvenated by a healthy diet and regular exercise, he appeared in an episode of the television series "Matt Houston." The 20 long, dark years of alcohol-and-pill addiction were over.

When Caesar later wrote about his long "black out" in his autobiography, he called the ordeal of alcoholism his "most humbling experience."

Sid Caesar, who appealed to a mass audience in his television series "Your Show of Shows" in the 1950s, overcame a barbiturate and alcohol problem after 20 years of addiction.

While Caesar was battling his drug addictions during the 1960s, a young comedian named Lenny Bruce was shocking and delighting audiences with his caustic, profane comments on American society, sex, drugs, and any other topic that was taboo, sensitive, or personal.

The product of a broken home, Bruce was reaching the peak of his comedic form during the early 1960s, the tail end of the Beat Movement in the United States. Beat artists had cast off the shackles of conformity and middle-class values. Their poems, novels, and music reflected their rejection of convention. Bruce's work appeared to mirror, in part, the Beat Movement's cynicsm toward mainstream America.

But Bruce's drug use and his uncompromising frankness — frequently expressed in obscenities — brought society's wrath down upon him. In September 1962, officials in Sydney, Australia, closed his show and banned him from television. A year later, British authorities banned him from entering England.

Lenny Bruce (left) leaves court with his lawyer in 1963. A brilliant and penetrating satirist, Bruce was prosecuted on both obscenity and drug-possession charges. He died in 1966 from a morphine overdose.

In describing an earlier performance by the comedian, a theater critic of England's *Evening Standard*, referred to Bruce's "liberal use of taboo words ... 3-letter, 4-letter, 7-letter and even a jumbo 12-letter word." The critic, however, did not write off the comedian as just a foul-mouthed Yankee. "Strip Mr. Bruce of his naughty syllables and we find that beneath his irreverent exterior there is an evangelist screaming to get out," the critic wrote. "He wants us to be honest about language, honest about religion, honest about prejudice, honest about sex."

Bruce had been arrested in Chicago on obscenity charges about a month before being banned from England; in April 1964 he was arrested in a nightclub in New York City's Greenwich Village.

Bruce's ability to perfom was being curtailed, and the New York arrest prompted a storm of protest by prominent artists (including the well-known writers James Jones, John Updike, Norman Mailer, and Allen Ginsberg). The artists signed a statement detailing their reasons for objecting to Bruce's arrest, describing the comedian as a social satirist "in the tradition of Swift, Rabelais, and Twain."

On November 4, 1964, the court convicted Lenny Bruce of giving an obscene performance. The vote was 2 to 1, with the dissenting judge holding that the obscenity laws were so vague that the question of defining community standards and obscenity might best be left to a federal constitutional convention.

The following year, on July 20, the California State District Court of Appeals reversed a lower court decision that had declared Bruce a narcotics addict. That decision would have committed the comedian to a state narcotics rehabilitation center for up to 10 years. It did not reverse his conviction in 1963 of heroin possession, which had led to Bruce's near-incarceration.

Although the reversal of the commitment was welcome news, Bruce still faced legal and financial troubles. On October 13 he filed suit as a pauper in the U.S. District Court in San Francisco, asking for an injunction against what he described as police harassment, which was interfering with his ability to make a living.

Virtually penniless by now, and officially declared a pauper by the court, Lenny Bruce opened at the Music Box theater in Hollywood in January 1966. That April he was given a suspended one-year jail term, fined $250, and put on two years' probation for the 1963 heroin conviction.

Probation kept him out of jail but not away from drugs. On August 3, 1966, he died in his home on Hollywood Boulevard. The police reported finding a hypodermic needle near his body. The Los Angeles County Coroner's office later ruled that Bruce had died of a morphine overdose.

About 10 years before his death Bruce had planted a tree in honor of his daughter Kitty. In 1977, the *Los Angeles Times* reported that another comedian, Freddie Prinze, had a leaf from that tree. The connection between the two comedians, though indirect, was made through a symbol of life. What the two comedians had in common, however, was a common abuse of drugs and a tragic, untimely death.

Prinze was born in 1954 and grew up in New York City. Already musically inclined, at 16 he entered the High School of Performing Arts where he began to study ballet. But his quick wit and way with a joke drew him toward comedy. His first big break came when he appeared at The Improvisation, a Manhattan nightclub. Prinze became successful very quickly after his debut, first with an appearance on Johnny Carson's "Tonight Show" and then as a co-star of the popular television comedy series "Chico and the Man."

But success came too fast for Prinze to handle it well. He looked to friends, relationships with women, and drugs for support and reassurance. The pressure of being the center of an entourage of managers, aides, and hangers-on, all more or less dependent on his success, also helped lead him to pills: stimulants to get him going in the morning and sedatives to help him sleep at night. He took a great deal of sedatives, especially Quaaludes.

A friend, comedian Jimmy Walker, told a newspaper, "Freddie was into a lot of drugs, not heroin, as far as I know, but coke and a lot of 'Ludes. The drug thing was a big part of Freddie's life. It completely messed him up."

Comedian David Brenner, who met Prinze when the doomed entertainer was only 17, confirmed to a reporter that Prinze "was dropping pills. I never saw him use heroin, but I know he used coke quite a bit." Brenner also got phone calls from Prinze around four in the morning, during which the troubled comedian, crying, would say things like, "I can't take it." Brenner felt that the jolt of success and the fast life of Los Angeles was too much for Prinze. Freddie's drug use kept increasing, finally totaling about $2,000 worth of cocaine a week, and six Quaaludes a day.

A final crushing blow to Prinze was the divorce from his wife of less than two years. Friends said the breakup itself did not bother him as much as the possibility of being separated from his son, 11-month-old Freddie. Prinze suffered greatly after the breakup. He cried, he lost weight, and he took drugs. On occasion he even showed friends a gun he owned and playfully discussed suicide.

In November 1976, while driving on a freeway near Van Nuys, California, he was stopped by a policeman who thought he was driving erratically. A blood test showed the presence of the tranquilizer methaqualone. The following January Prinze pleaded guilty to the misdemeanor charge of driving while under the influence of drugs. He did not live to go to trial.

Everything finally came apart on the night of January 28, 1977. Prinze was sitting in his apartment in the Beverly Comstock Hotel in Los Angeles with his business agent, Marvin Snyder. The troubled comedian called his former wife on the phone. The conversation seemed to disturb him. Prinze hung up the phone, reached under the sofa cushions on which he was sitting, and grabbed a gun. Then he put the weapon to his head and fired.

Prinze died 33 hours later at the University of California–Los Angeles Medical Center. His will left the bulk of his estate to his mother and to his son, Freddie, Jr.

Luckier than Prinze was Richard Pryor, who began his sometimes-turbulent life on December 1, 1940, in Peoria, Illinois. He spent his early years with his grandmother, who operated a house of prostitution there. His parents had divorced and each had remarried, but it was left to his grandmother to raise him. Although he saw the raw edges of life as he grew up — including, of course, racism — Pryor was also protected by his loving grandmother and her friends. Pryor began his career in comedy in the 1960s. He toured the Midwest for a while, then headed for New York City. In 1965 he appeared on Merv Griffin's new talk show and, later that year, on "The Ed Sullivan Show." Superstardom seemed to be within reach.

Yet by 1976 Pryor was coming "unglued," according to a biography of the comedian written by Jim Haskins. In his book *Richard Pryor: A Man and His Madness*, Haskins wrote that Pryor was uncomfortable with his success. He felt guilty and undeserving of it because of his background as a poor black growing up in a world of vice.

"Deep down," wrote Haskins, "he felt like a fake, as if at any moment the hoax might be discovered. In part, he was indeed faking. He was beginning to feel constricted doing the type of comedy material he was forced to perform in order to be acceptable on television, or even in the Las Vegas clubs where he was now getting bookings for three thousand dollars a week. . . . Cocaine seemed to be his only friend. By his own admission he was a heavy user at this time, having graduated from marijuana, although he still smoked reefers on occasion. . . . Pryor says now that cocaine was the cause of a lot of the trouble he got into during that period of his life."

In addition, Pryor drank heavily, which, or course, contributed to his problems. He continued to appear in movies during the 1970s, and he gave live concerts. But past marriages and divorces had left their scars — as well as several children he seldom saw. And much of his money was going to drugs. On the night of June 9, 1980, his expensive cocaine habit nearly cost him his life.

Pryor has given conflicting accounts of the near-fatal accident that resulted in his being burned over 50% of his body. He first claimed that the accident occurred while he was "free-basing" cocaine, a method of smoking purified cocaine in which a mixture of cocaine and ether is heated and the fumes inhaled. But in 1986 he admitted to television journalist Barbara Walters that he had lied about the free-basing. What really happened, he claimed, was that — driven to despair over his cocaine addiction — he had poured rum all over himself on fire in an effort to commit suicide. Although he was no longer abusing cocaine and alcohol, he explained, he could never stop attending meetings of Alcoholics Anonymous if he was to retain control over his addictions.

John Belushi in the successful comedy film Animal House. *Although the star's death from an overdose of heroin and cocaine in 1982 shocked the world, his friends and colleagues had known of his heavy drug use for several years.*

Despite the severity of his injuries, Pryor was able to leave the hospital about a month and a half after the fire, very thankful to be alive.

The following August he began his comeback: a live performance at the Comedy Store on Sunset Strip in Los Angeles. The film version of that show, *Richard Pryor: Live on the Sunset Strip*, was a hit. And in 1986 he starred in *JoJo Dancer, Your Life Is Calling*, a film based largely on his own life.

Not all Pryor's contemporaries were that fortunate. The year after Pryor's comeback, drugs claimed another victim. News of this death spread like a shock wave on March 5, 1982.

John Belushi was dead.

Dan Ackroyd, his friend and co-star in movies and on the television comedy show "Saturday Night Live," got the news by telephone in his office in New York City. Ackroyd left the office and went to Belushi's New York apartment to tell the dead comedian's wife, Judy, so she would not first hear about it on a news broadcast.

Comedian Robin Williams, shown here with his wife Valerie, allegedly took cocaine with John Belushi on the night of his death. Williams later wondered if he could have done something to save his friend and colleague.

The comedian Robin Williams, who had visited Belushi's bungalow at the Chateau Marmont Hotel in Hollywood the previous night, heard the news when he was on the set of his television show, "Mork and Mindy." Williams left the set, according to Bob Woodward's book *Wired: The Short Life and Fast Times of John Belushi*, and walked to a back-lot street of Paramount studios. He knew Belushi had been heavily involved with drugs; according to Woodward's account, he had even shared a little cocaine with Belushi the night before. Now he wondered if he could have done something to prevent this tragedy.

Dr. Ronald Kornblum, the deputy medical examiner for the City of Los Angeles, performed the autopsy on Belushi's body the following morning. His conclusion: death from respiratory failure brought on by an overdose of a mixture of cocaine and heroin. (Injecting such a mixture is called "speed-balling"; the cocaine gives a quick, intense high, while the heroin eases the intense depression that ensues once the effect of the cocaine wears off.)

Even before the autopsy an investigator for the coroner's office had discovered needle marks on the inside of both of Belushi's elbows—a sure sign of drug abuse.

Four years later a Los Angeles judge sentenced Cathy Evelyn Smith to three years in prison for supplying "the poison" that killed Belushi. Smith had earlier admitted to a reporter that she had injected Belushi with heroin and cocaine over the last few days of his life.

Although people were shocked at the comedian's death, Belushi's friends had known of his drug problem for quite a while.

According to *Saturday Night: A Backstage History of Saturday Night Live*, by 1976, the program's second season, Belushi was ingesting "massive amounts of cocaine."

During the first year of the show Belushi was very competitive with another, more popular performer, Chevy Chase. Chase left the show after the first year, married, and moved to Hollywood. During that time he went through a period of heavy cocaine and alcohol abuse. Some witnesses said later that he often consumed over two grams of cocaine a day, an amount that left him swinging between megalomania and paranoia; at one point Chase was virtually incoherent. His wife sued for divorce.

Although Chase evidently cut down on his cocaine use, he later faced another drug problem. In October 1986, he checked into the Betty Ford Center to kick his dependence on the prescription painkillers he had started taking for back pain — a legacy from the pratfalls and stunts he had performed over the years, dating back to "Saturday Night Live."

Once Chase left the show there was no one to overshadow Belushi, and Belushi became aggressively confident, sometimes arrogant toward fellow performers. He increased his use of drugs. Unlike some comedians, such as Sid Caesar and Richard Pryor, Belushi apparently harbored no serious guilt about his success or insecurity about his talent. He was bold, brash, and confident. He was very funny and very popular. Perhaps his friends and business associates simply did not want to interfere with their important and successful friend because they feared he would turn on them in anger.

In this regard, actor Treat Williams voiced a significant self-indictment of his own failure to intervene in Belushi's self-destructive drug abuse. As quoted in *Wired*, Williams said: "It takes a real good friend to say 'Stop.' If you do, perhaps you'll lose a friend. I wasn't strong enough, man enough, to say it. I think people are afraid of the commitment in getting involved in someone else's life, even if they're ending it before your eyes."

The Betty Ford Rehabilitation Center was founded by Mrs. Ford after she herself had overcome drug dependence. The center has helped many celebrities battle addiction and regain control over their lives.

CHAPTER 6

DEGLAMORIZING DRUGS

In response to growing pressure from many quarters, the entertainment industry has responded to the problem of drug abuse within its ranks by making counseling programs more easily available to their employees who have drug abuse problems. In the 1980s Metro Goldwin Mayer/United Artists, the American Broadcasting Company, and the American Federation of Television and Radio Artists set up their own programs for employees with drug abuse problems. The Federation's program, the Broadcast and Recording Industry Council on Alcoholism, expanded its services to deal with drug abuse problems in addition to alcoholism.

On April 11, 1984, approximately 125 representatives of the entertainment industry, including men and women from unions and television and production companies, attended a conference at the Burbank Studios in Burbank, California. The conference was designed to stimulate interest in establishing an industrywide employee assistance program (EAP) to provide counseling, referral, and education to drug abusers on a confidential basis.

Columbia Pictures, Warner Brothers, and the Scott Newman Foundation (later changed to the Scott Newman Foundation Center) sponsored the conference. The Scott Newman Foundation Center in Pasadena, California, is affiliated with the Health Behavior Research Institute of the School of Pharmacy at the University of Southern California. Actor Paul Newman established the center in 1981 following the death of his son Scott from an accidental overdose of Valium and alcohol in 1979. The center assists the entertainment industry in producing movies and television programs that demonstrate realistically the dangers of drug abuse. The center provides technical advisory service and sometimes assists in plot development.

One of the principal speakers at the 1984 conference that the center cosponsored with Columbia and Warner Brothers was Betty Ford.

Another speaker, actor Ralph Waite, star of the television program "The Waltons," and also a recovered alcoholic, said at the conference that he had been drunk when he was hired to play the role of the father on "The Waltons" and kept a "stash of vodka and grapefruit juice" on the set every day for the first three months of the program. He also admitted that the disruption caused by his drinking during the first movie he ever made cost the production company, $75,000.

In September 1984 the employee assistance program that had been proposed during the Burbank conference was established in that city. Called the Entertainment Industry Referral and Assistance Center (EIRAC), it is a confidential, nonprofit, industry-wide program funded by major studios, television networks unions, and other organizations and individuals as a service to industry employees and their families.

By mid-1986 EIRAC was receiving 40 calls each month from members of the industry looking for help, or from supervisors calling to refer an employee because that employee's job performance was unsatisfactory owing to drug abuse. (Although some employees or their families require marital or psychological counseling rather than drug rehabilitation, the majority of calls are in response to a drug problem.)

EIRAC is staffed by professionals who evaluate drug and alcohol problems among clients and determine the appropriate measures to help them. The staff then refers clients to appropriate medical facilities, outpatient services, counseling, or self-help groups. EIRAC assists clients who lack adequate medical insurance to minimize costs by making referrals to the most appropriate agencies, some of which charge according to how much the client is able to pay.

Although industry employees with a drug problem are not required to contact EIRAC, the incentive to use its services is great. If the employee's performance continues to be unsatisfactory, he or she can be fired. The referral center thus offers industry employees a cure for their job-threatening drug problem.

Despite a nationwide antidrug spirit that gained momentum toward the end of the 1980s, the number of artists with drug problems is increasing, according to Tom Kenny, who runs drug treatment programs in the Los Angeles area. Kenny is the director of Studio 12, a residential alcohol-and-drug program in North Hollywood that cares for members of the entertainment industry, including writers, actors, camera operators, and other artists and technical advisors. Founded in November 1980, Studio 12 had treated more than 500 people by mid-1986.

The problem of cocaine addiction became so serious that in January 1983 Kenny founded Cocaine Anonymous (CA), based on the principles of Alcoholics Anonymous, including regular meetings for cocaine users and former users.

Within three years after Kenny founded CA in North Hollywood, the program encompassed more than 100 weekly meetings in Los Angeles alone, as well as meetings in 30 states and England. Although CA is open to the public, Kenny estimates that about 15% to 20% of the people who attend the meetings work in the entertainment industry.

Despite the existence of such programs, Kenny claims that as of 1986 the problem was worse than ever. One of the reasons cited by Kenny for the worsening problem was the appearance of crack. This particularly addictive form of cocaine appealed to some people in the entertainment industry who worked long hours, sometimes 15 to 17 hours a day, during which there were often long periods of boredom.

Their answer to boredom was crack, and their response to crack was addiction.

In addition, the so-called pyramid scheme has produced large numbers of users. Cocaine abusers who need more money to feed their addiction become dealers, attracting still more people to the drug. And some of those new customers become addicted, become dealers, and spread the addiction to still more people.

That expanding problem, of course, is not restricted to Hollywood. Any city is fair game and must respond accordingly. In New York City, for example, the Performing Arts Center for Health (PACH) offers psychiatric and medical counseling and referral services to performing artists. The psychiatric service, which is part of New York University Medical Center/Bellevue Hospital, responds to all psychiatric needs, including drug abuse.

PACH, which refers performing artists to clinics that charge reduced rates for their services, was established in 1981. Among the founders were two former ballet dancers, one of whom became a health writer for *Dancemagazine.*

The year they founded PACH, that writer, Marian Horosko, published a series of articles on drug abuse in the magazine. The articles described the social conditions contributing to drug abuse and offered advice to dancers on how to deal with personal and professional pressures without resorting to drugs, which, the article pointed out, can cause "a crashing despondency, fatigue, and sadness afterwards." Drug use "has been the death knell for rock stars and athletes, as well as dancers," Horosko concluded.

Ballet dancer Gelsey Kirkland gave dramatic support to that thesis with her 1986 book, *Dancing on My Grave,* the story of her fall from the heights of stardom to the depths of cocaine addiction.

Kirkland's foray into educating the public in the fine points of drug abuse in the arts was one of a number of attempts by performers in various fields to use their celebrity status to deglamorize drugs — and by doing so, to take a stand among their peers against drugs.

Rock musician Stevie Wonder, for example, laid it on the line with his song "Don't Drive Drunk." The blind performer backed up his lyrics by appearing on a poster that showed his face under the quote, "Before I'll ride with a drunk, I'll drive myself."

In 1986 a campaign called Rock Against Drugs used former drug-abusing rock celebrities in a series of video spots to run on the cable-television channels MTV and VH-1 (rock-music-video stations), and Nickelodeon. Funds to support the campaign came from MTV Networks Entertainment, owner

Gelsey Kirkland dances with her most famous partner, Mikhail Baryshnikov. Kirkland's autobiography, Dancing on My Grave, *describes how cocaine dependence almost destroyed her career.*

of those channels, as well as the California Attorney General's Office and the Pepsi-Cola Company.

Danny Goldberg, the campaign's executive, announced that musicians, directors, and producers, some of whom were former drug abusers, volunteered their time for the campaign. One of the volunteers, Steve Jones, former lead guitarist with the Sex Pistols, explained his commitment to the project by saying that he had stopped using drugs a short time before; he now wanted to help prevent young people from becoming involved with drugs.

"That really is the whole thing," he told a reporter for United Press International. "If you can save one mind, you've done something."

Another volunteer, Vince Neil of Mötley Crüe, filmed a television spot sitting on a motorcycle. "Don't get me wrong," he says as he looks out at the audience. "I still party with the best of them. Now I do it without drugs."

Other rock artists who volunteered to appear in spots were Bob Seger, Lou Reed, Dee Snyder of Twisted Sister, Gene Simmons of Kiss, and Belinda Carlisle.

Meanwhile, the ascendancy of crack has prompted leading musical artists to form Artists for Crack Education (ACE), an educational program in New York City. Supported by the Crack-Down Fund, ACE was created to bring artists from the entertainment industry who could serve as positive role models to work with crack abuse specialists and to speak at New York City schools and drug-rehabilitation centers; to produce public service announcements featuring celebrities to be made available to the Board of Education, radio and television stations, and other institutions nationwide; and to provide the Board of Education with funds for additional crack-awareness programs.

As part of the fund-raising effort the Crack-Down Fund sponsored a two-day "Crack-Down" concert in New York featuring such major stars as Rubén Blades and his band, the rap group Run-D.M.C., Santana, a reunited Crosby, Stills & Nash, and a temporarily reunited Allman Brothers Band. Both

Run-D.M.C. members Darryl McDaniels (left) and Jason Mizzell are among several rock musicians who are speaking openly about the dangers of substance abuse, urging young people to say "no" to drugs.

the Allman Brothers Band and Crosby, Stills & Nash had previously had major drug problems that contributed to the breakup of their bands. (See Chapter 2.)

Run-D.M.C., a much more recent group, had already made a point of saying in one of their raps, "We are not thugs/ We don't use drugs."

The Alcohol and Drug Abuse Committee of the Caucus for Producers, Writers, and Directors also joined the campaign against drugs. The caucus sent a memo to members of these professions following an accident in which a drunk driver slammed into a car in which stage and movie stars Mary Martin and Janet Gaynor, and two of their friends, Paul Gregory and Ben Washer, were riding. Washer was killed in the September 5, 1982, accident, and both Martin and Gaynor were seriously injured. The memo prepared by the caucus read in part:

> We of the Caucus for Producers, Writers and Directors, have done some thinking. Have any of us as members of the creative community in Hollywood unwittingly glorified the casual use of alcohol in one of our projects? Have we written it as macho? Directed it as cute? Produced it as an accepted way of life? In short, are we subliminally putting a label of "perfectly okay" on alcohol-related behavior and selling it to the American people? . . . . The answer, we fear, is yes. Alcohol is the number-one drug of choice in the United States. The consequences of its misuse are not cute, macho, or acceptable.

The memo concluded with suggestions to modify the portrayal of alcohol abuse as acceptable or desirable. For example, it urged that drinking should not be glamorized or associated with "macho pursuits."

The National Association of Broadcasters Task Force on Alcohol and Drug Abuse also began an alcohol-awareness drive. In 1985 the task force provided drunk driving and alcohol-abuse public-service announcements for radio and television stations. Its 1986 theme, "Celebrate Sober," was aimed at reducing alcohol-related automobile accidents during the period of high-school and college graduations.

Starting in 1983, the National Institute on Drug Abuse (NIDA) and the Advertising Council produced a series of antidrug public service announcements for television. These "Just Say No" campaigns were designed to encourage young people to resist peer pressure to take drugs. In February 1985 the campaign introduced a music video, "Schoolyard," which NIDA began lending to schools and organizations. The video depicts an older boy helping a young boy say "no" to a drug pusher.

First Lady Nancy Reagan was deeply involved in the campaign and visited schools and drug-rehabilitation centers around the country listening and talking to young students and former drug abusers. In 1986 the Charles A. Dana foundation gave her a special award for what it described as her "outstanding achievements in educating young people throughout the land and around the world to the major health problem of drug abuse and challenging them to organize to prevent it."

Mrs. Reagan was host of the 1983 television special "The Chemical People," a two-part series produced by WQED, the public television station in Pittsburgh, Pennsylvania. The series treated drug abuse as a health problem and urged viewers to rally community support to fight drug abuse.

Parents, students, and teachers watched the program in town halls and gymnasiums around the country, and many more watched the program on television. The public viewings were held to encourage community action in combating drug abuse.

In 1986 Mrs. Reagan was the keynote speaker at a two-day drug-abuse conference sponsored by the Academy of Television Arts and Sciences. In a luncheon speech she told television officials, "Kids are very vulnerable to the power of suggestion, and that's exactly where television is supreme."

Although he insisted that the television industry has never actively encouraged drug abuse, Richard Frank, president of the academy, said that television has perhaps publicized and at times glamorized drug abuse as part of an exciting life-style.

During the 1980s, television has contributed to the drug-education campaign by airing episodes of popular television series with antidrug story lines. Episodes of several ABC se-

First Lady Nancy Reagan, who has played a significant role in the national campaign against drug abuse, was honored for her efforts by the Sportscasters' Hall of Fame in 1986.

ries, such as "Hotel," "Happy Days," and "Dynasty," deglamorized drug use. A leading character on "Hotel" became addicted to painkillers in one episode; after failing to quit her habit, she sought help. A student on "Happy Days" became addicted to sleeping pills and received counseling that helped her to overcome her habit. And a recurring story on "Dynasty" during the 1984 season was the deterioration of a character who became addicted to cocaine.

In the 1982 made-for-television movie *Dreams Don't Die*, a young man living in an inner-city neighborhood helped the police break up a drug ring terrorizing the local kids. A continuing story line in the CBS series "Cagney and Lacey" explored the effect of cocaine use on Chris Cagney's boyfriend and the effect his problem had on their relationship; later episodes found Cagney trying to help her father acknowledge and deal with his alcoholism. A recurring story line on "Falcon Crest" also explored the deterioration of a regular character who was addicted to cocaine.

Another CBS series, "Dallas," reduced scenes portraying alcohol consumption by 70% according to a network executive who testified before the 1985 Senate subcommittee hearing on the entertainment industry's role in deglamorizing drugs.

Following the airing of the CBS made-for-television movie *Not My Kid*, about the ordeal of the parents of a 15-year-old girl who abuses drugs and commits crimes to support her habit, more than 500 calls for help came in to one drug treatment center alone, according to Dr. Carlton E. Turner, Special Assistant to the President for Drug Abuse Policy.

The 1986 CBS made-for-television movie *Courage*, starring Sophia Loren as the mother of a young boy who becomes a drug addict, was based on a true story. The woman's son had progressed from cocaine to heroin abuse, and she felt helpless to do anything. Her despair turned to outrage when she discovered a family friend was involved in the cocaine trade. The woman went to the drug authorities and offered to work undercover to help them catch the criminals. In real life, the woman's efforts are said to have helped break a $3.5 billion cocaine ring.

In 1981 NBC, in cooperation with Paramount Pictures, aired a special week-long series of antidrug commercials as part of its Get High on Yourself campaign. The series began with a one-hour special featuring a variety of celebrities, including rock star Ted Nugent. Film Producer Robert Evans undertook the project as one condition of his probation after being convicted of cocaine possession.

Among the regular NBC programs that deglamorized drugs were "Knight Rider," which in one episode depicted the death of a rock singer from a drug overdose; "The Facts of Life," in which a boy admits to his girl friend that he would rather spend his time and money on drugs than on her; and "The Cosby Show," in which parents confront their son after finding a marijuana cigarette in his schoolbook but believe him when he says that someone else must have put it there when he was in school. The son finds the boy responsible for doing it and brings the student home as proof to his parents that he is innocent. The show's star, comedian Bill

Cosby, prefaced one of the programs in 1986 with a warning to young people to avoid drugs.

The growing role of the entertainment industry in drug-awareness programs seems to reflect, in part, the chastening experiences of those celebrities who suffered physical and professional damage because of their own drug problems. By helping to publicize rather than hide their problems, celebrities helped spread the word about the dangers of recreational drug use.

One of those celebrities, actress Elizabeth Taylor, took responsibility for her drug addictions with a particularly harsh self-indictment. She made her remarks in 1985 during an interview with the *New York Times* after her release from the Betty Ford Center. Her words reflect the courage she had to muster to face her problem and the determination she had to have to overcome her addictions: "Drunk is a hard word, but I've had to be hard with myself to face it. . . . Somebody who drinks too much is a drunk. Somebody who takes too many pills is a junkie. There's no polite way of saying it."

APPENDIX

State Agencies
for the Prevention and Treatment
of Drug Abuse

ALABAMA
Department of Mental Health
Division of Mental Illness and
  Substance Abuse Community
  Programs
200 Interstate Park Drive
P.O. Box 3710
Montgomery, AL 36193
(205) 271-9253

ALASKA
Department of Health and Social
  Services
Office of Alcoholism and Drug
  Abuse
Pouch H-05-F
Juneau, AK 99811
(907) 586-6201

ARIZONA
Department of Health Services
Division of Behavioral Health
  Services
Bureau of Community Services
Alcohol Abuse and Alcoholism
  Section
2500 East Van Buren
Phoenix, AZ 85008
(602) 255-1238

Department of Health Services
Division of Behavioral Health
  Services
Bureau of Community Services
Drug Abuse Section
2500 East Van Buren
Phoenix, AZ 85008
(602) 255-1240

ARKANSAS
Department of Human Services
Office of Alcohol and Drug Abuse
  Prevention
1515 West 7th Avenue
Suite 310
Little Rock, AR 72202
(501) 371-2603

CALIFORNIA
Department of Alcohol and Drug
  Abuse
111 Capitol Mall
Sacramento, CA 95814
(916) 445-1940

COLORADO
Department of Health
Alcohol and Drug Abuse Division
4210 East 11th Avenue
Denver, CO 80220
(303) 320-6137

CONNECTICUT
Alcohol and Drug Abuse
  Commission
999 Asylum Avenue
3rd Floor
Hartford, CT 06105
(203) 566-4145

DELAWARE
Division of Mental Health
Bureau of Alcoholism and Drug
  Abuse
1901 North Dupont Highway
Newcastle, DE 19720
(302) 421-6101

DISTRICT OF COLUMBIA
Department of Human Services
Office of Health Planning and
  Development
601 Indiana Avenue, NW
Suite 500
Washington, D.C. 20004
(202) 724-5641

FLORIDA
Department of Health and
  Rehabilitative Services
Alcoholic Rehabilitation Program
1317 Winewood Boulevard
Room 187A
Tallahassee, FL 32301
(904) 488-0396

Department of Health and
  Rehabilitative Services
Drug Abuse Program
1317 Winewood Boulevard
Building 6, Room 155
Tallahassee, FL 32301
(904) 488-0900

GEORGIA
Department of Human Resources
Division of Mental Health and
  Mental Retardation
Alcohol and Drug Section
618 Ponce De Leon Avenue, NE
Atlanta, GA 30365-2101
(404) 894-4785

HAWAII
Department of Health
Mental Health Division
Alcohol and Drug Abuse Branch
1250 Punch Bowl Street
P.O. Box 3378
Honolulu, HI 96801
(808) 548-4280

IDAHO
Department of Health and Welfare
Bureau of Preventive Medicine
Substance Abuse Section
450 West State
Boise, ID 83720
(208) 334-4368

ILLINOIS
Department of Mental Health and
  Developmental Disabilities
Division of Alcoholism
160 North La Salle Street
Room 1500
Chicago, IL 60601
(312) 793-2907

Illinois Dangerous Drugs
  Commission
300 North State Street
Suite 1500
Chicago, IL 60610
(312) 822-9860

INDIANA
Department of Mental Health
Division of Addiction Services
429 North Pennsylvania Street
Indianapolis, IN 46204
(317) 232-7816

IOWA
Department of Substance Abuse
505 5th Avenue
Insurance Exchange Building
Suite 202
Des Moines, IA 50319
(515) 281-3641

KANSAS
Department of Social Rehabilitation
Alcohol and Drug Abuse Services
2700 West 6th Street
Biddle Building
Topeka, KS 66606
(913) 296-3925

KENTUCKY
Cabinet for Human Resources
Department of Health Services
Substance Abuse Branch
275 East Main Street
Frankfort, KY 40601
(502) 564-2880

LOUISIANA
Department of Health and Human
  Resources
Office of Mental Health and
  Substance Abuse
655 North 5th Street
P.O. Box 4049
Baton Rouge, LA 70821
(504) 342-2565

MAINE
Department of Human Services
Office of Alcoholism and Drug
  Abuse Prevention
Bureau of Rehabilitation
32 Winthrop Street
Augusta, ME 04330
(207) 289-2781

MARYLAND
Alcoholism Control Administration
201 West Preston Street
Fourth Floor
Baltimore, MD 21201
(301) 383-2977

State Health Department
Drug Abuse Administration
201 West Preston Street
Baltimore, MD 21201
(301) 383-3312

MASSACHUSETTS
Department of Public Health
Division of Alcoholism
755 Boylston Street
Sixth Floor
Boston, MA 02116
(617) 727-1960

Department of Public Health
Division of Drug Rehabilitation
600 Washington Street
Boston, MA 02114
(617) 727-8617

MICHIGAN
Department of Public Health
Office of Substance Abuse Services
3500 North Logan Street
P.O. Box 30035
Lansing, MI 48909
(517) 373-8603

MINNESOTA
Department of Public Welfare
Chemical Dependency Program
  Division
Centennial Building
658 Cedar Street
4th Floor
Saint Paul, MN 55155
(612) 296-4614

MISSISSIPPI
Department of Mental Health
Division of Alcohol and Drug Abuse
1102 Robert E. Lee Building
Jackson, MS 39201
(601) 359-1297

MISSOURI
Department of Mental Health
Division of Alcoholism and Drug
  Abuse
2002 Missouri Boulevard
P.O. Box 687
Jefferson City, MO 65102
(314) 751-4942

MONTANA
Department of Institutions
Alcohol and Drug Abuse Division
1539 11th Avenue
Helena, MT 59620
(406) 449-2827

NEBRASKA
Department of Public Institutions
Division of Alcoholism and Drug
Abuse
801 West Van Dorn Street
P.O. Box 94728
Lincoln, NB 68509
(402) 471-2851, Ext. 415

NEVADA
Department of Human Resources
Bureau of Alcohol and Drug Abuse
505 East King Street
Carson City, NV 89710
(702) 885-4790

NEW HAMPSHIRE
Department of Health and Welfare
Office of Alcohol and Drug Abuse
   Prevention
Hazen Drive
Health and Welfare Building
Concord, NH 03301
(603) 271-4627

NEW JERSEY
Department of Health
Division of Alcoholism
129 East Hanover Street CN 362
Trenton, NJ 08625
(609) 292-8949

Department of Health
Division of Narcotic and Drug
   Abuse Control
129 East Hanover Street CN 362
Trenton, NJ 08625
(609) 292-8949

NEW MEXICO
Health and Environment Department
Behavioral Services Division
Substance Abuse Bureau
725 Saint Michaels Drive
P.O. Box 968
Santa Fe, NM 87503
(505) 984-0020, Ext. 304

NEW YORK
Division of Alcoholism and Alcohol
   Abuse
194 Washington Avenue
Albany, NY 12210
(518) 474-5417

Division of Substance Abuse
   Services
Executive Park South
Box 8200
Albany, NY 12203
(518) 457-7629

NORTH CAROLINA
Department of Human Resources
Division of Mental Health, Mental
   Retardation and Substance Abuse
   Services
Alcohol and Drug Abuse Services
325 North Salisbury Street
Albemarle Building
Raleigh, NC 27611
(919) 733-4670

NORTH DAKOTA
Department of Human Services
Division of Alcoholism and Drug
   Abuse
State Capitol Building
Bismarck, ND 58505
(701) 224-2767

OHIO
Department of Health
Division of Alcoholism
246 North High Street
P.O. Box 118
Columbus, OH 43216
(614) 466-3543

Department of Mental Health
Bureau of Drug Abuse
65 South Front Street
Columbus, OH 43215
(614) 466-9023

OKLAHOMA
Department of Mental Health
Alcohol and Drug Programs
4545 North Lincoln Boulevard
Suite 100 East Terrace
P.O. Box 53277
Oklahoma City, OK 73152
(405) 521-0044

OREGON
Department of Human Resources
Mental Health Division
Office of Programs for Alcohol and
Drug Problems
2575 Bittern Street, NE
Salem, OR 97310
(503) 378-2163

PENNSYLVANIA
Department of Health
Office of Drug and Alcohol
Programs
Commonwealth and Forster Avenues
Health and Welfare Building
P.O. Box 90
Harrisburg, PA 17108
(717) 787-9857

RHODE ISLAND
Department of Mental Health,
Mental Retardation and Hospitals
Division of Substance Abuse
Substance Abuse Administration
Building
Cranston, RI 02920
(401) 464-2091

SOUTH CAROLINA
Commission on Alcohol and Drug
Abuse
3700 Forest Drive
Columbia, SC 29204
(803) 758-2521

SOUTH DAKOTA
Department of Health
Division of Alcohol and Drug Abuse
523 East Capitol, Joe Foss Building
Pierre, SD 57501
(605) 773-4806

TENNESSEE
Department of Mental Health and
Mental Retardation
Alcohol and Drug Abuse Services
505 Deaderick Street
James K. Polk Building,
Fourth Floor
Nashville, TN 37219
(615) 741-1921

TEXAS
Commission on Alcoholism
809 Sam Houston State Office
Building
Austin, TX 78701
(512) 475-2577
Department of Community Affairs
Drug Abuse Prevention Division
2015 South Interstate Highway 35
P.O. Box 13166
Austin, TX 78711
(512) 443-4100

UTAH
Department of Social Services
Division of Alcoholism and Drugs
150 West North Temple
Suite 350
P.O. Box 2500
Salt Lake City, UT 84110
(801) 533-6532

VERMONT
Agency of Human Services
Department of Social and
Rehabilitation Services
Alcohol and Drug Abuse Division
103 South Main Street
Waterbury, VT 05676
(802) 241-2170

VIRGINIA
Department of Mental Health and
  Mental Retardation
Division of Substance Abuse
109 Governor Street
P.O. Box 1797
Richmond, VA 23214
(804) 786-5313

WASHINGTON
Department of Social and Health
  Service
Bureau of Alcohol and Substance
  Abuse
Office Building—44 W
Olympia, WA 98504
(206) 753-5866

WEST VIRGINIA
Department of Health
Office of Behavioral Health Services
Division on Alcoholism and Drug
  Abuse
1800 Washington Street East
Building 3 Room 451
Charleston, WV 25305
(304) 348-2276

WISCONSIN
Department of Health and Social
  Services
Division of Community Services
Bureau of Community Programs
Alcohol and Other Drug Abuse
  Program Office
1 West Wilson Street
P.O. Box 7851
Madison, WI 53707
(608) 266-2717

WYOMING
Alcohol and Drug Abuse Programs
Hathaway Building
Cheyenne, WY 82002
(307) 777-7115, Ext. 7118

GUAM
Mental Health & Substance Abuse
  Agency
P.O. Box 20999
Guam 96921

PUERTO RICO
Department of Addiction Control
  Services
Alcohol Abuse Programs
P.O. Box B-Y Rio Piedras Station
Rio Piedras, PR 00928
(809) 763-5014

Department of Addiction Control
  Services
Drug Abuse Programs
P.O. Box B-Y Rio Piedras Station
Rio Piedras, PR 00928
(809) 764-8140

VIRGIN ISLANDS
Division of Mental Health,
  Alcoholism & Drug Dependency
  Services
P.O. Box 7329
Saint Thomas, Virgin Islands 00801
(809) 774-7265

AMERICAN SAMOA
LBJ Tropical Medical Center
Department of Mental Health Clinic
Pago Pago, American Samoa 96799

TRUST TERRITORIES
Director of Health Services
Office of the High Commissioner
Saipan, Trust Territories 96950

Further Reading

Abel, Ernest L. *Marijuana: The First Twelve Thousand Years*. New York: McGraw Hill, 1982.

Anger, Kenneth. *Hollywood Babylon*. New York: E. P. Dutton, 1984.

Pareles, Jon and Patricia Romanski, eds. *The Rolling Stone Encyclopedia of Rock & Roll*. New York: Rolling Stone Press/Summit Books, 1983.

Shaw, Arnold. *Dictionary of American Pop/Rock*. New York: Schirmer Books/Macmillan, 1982.

Whitcomb, Ian. *After the Ball: Pop Music from Rag to Rock*. New York: Simon & Schuster, 1972.

Whitcomb, Ian. *Rock Odyssey*. New York: Doubleday, 1983.

Glossary

acute referring to a condition in which the symptoms are often severe but of short duration and often rapid onset

addiction a condition caused by repeated drug use, characterized by a compulsive urge to continue using the drug, a tendency to increase the dosage, and physiological and/or psychological dependence

alkaloid one of many organic substances that contain nitrogen and strongly affect body functions; drugs such as morphine and cocaine are alkaloids

amphetamine a drug that stimulates the nervous system; generally used as a mood elevator, energizer, antidepressant, and appetite suppressant

anesthetic a drug that produces loss of sensation, sometimes accompanied by loss of consciousness

antidepressant any one of a number of substances that alleviate symptoms of severe depression

barbiturate a drug that causes depression of the central nervous system, generally used to reduce anxiety or to induce euphoria

Beat movement a cultural movement in the 1950s in which people expressed a nonconformist social philosophy by the way they dressed and behaved

cardiac arrhythmia irregular heart rhythm induced by physiological or pathological dysfunctions; in its extreme form, cardiac arrhythmia is synonymous to a heart attack

celebrity a well-known person often discussed by the media

chronic referring to a long-term condition or disease, often of gradual onset

cocaine the primary psychoactive ingredient in the coca plant; it functions as a behavioral stimulant

cold turkey the process of withdrawing suddenly and without the help of therapeutic aids from a highly addictive drug

crack a highly addictive and extremely dangerous form of cocaine that is smoked so the user can achieve a "high"

decadence a state of deterioration

133

deglamorization making unattractive or less romantic or alluring

derelict a person who is abandoned or drops out of society, no longer follows conventional social mores or standards, and is unable to support himself

detoxification the body's process for removing poisonous substances or rendering them harmless; the liver often performs this function

dissipation the state of having squandered something of value; also, the extravagant pursuit of pleasure, particularly alcohol or drug abuse, at the expense of personal health

endorphins compounds produced in the brain that serve as the body's natural opiates; similar to enkephalins

euphoria a mental high characterized by a sense of well-being

freebasing a potent and dangerous method of drug abuse in which street cocaine is mixed with ammonium hydroxide and heated, then smoked in a pipe for a quick and addictive high

hallucinogenic producing sensory impressions that have no basis in reality; some drugs such as LSD can be hallucinogenic

Huntington's chorea an inherited disease affecting the central nervous system, characterized by jerky involuntary movements and causing dementia and progressive deterioration of posture

jazz a type of music that originated in the United States characterized by rhythm and an improvisational beat

junkie someone physically addicted to a drug, often an opiate; slang expression

marijuana the leaves, flowers, buds, and/or branches of the hemp plant that contain cannabinoids, a group of intoxicating drugs

narcotic a drug that produces sleep and relieves pain in small doses but causes stupors and unconsciousness in larger amounts; examples are opium, codeine, morphine, and heroin

nihilism rejection of existing moral, cultural, and religious beliefs

opiate any compound from the milky juice of the poppy plant *Papaver somniferum*, including opium, morphine, codeine, and their derivatives, such as heroin

overdose ingestion of a drug, or a combination of drugs, that leads to extreme physical reactions that can include coma or even death

physical dependence adaption of the body to the presence of a drug so that its absence produces withdrawal symptoms

Prohibition the period from 1920 to 1933, during which the manufacture and sale of liquor in the United States was illegal

psychedelic producing hallucinations or having mind-altering or mind-expanding properties

psychological dependence a condition in which the drug user craves a drug to maintain a sense of well-being and feels discomfort when deprived of it

psychosis an extreme mental disorder characterized by a loss of contact with reality, hallucinations, and delusions

punk rock a type of music characterized by violent nihilistic lyrics and linked to bizarre dress and behavior of musicians

rehabilitation training that enables a person to return to and function in daily life after a period of imprisonment or illness

rhythm & blues a type of music characterized by strong rhythms and the sad, jazzy melodies associated with "blues" music

speedball a combination of heroin and cocaine

tolerance a decrease of susceptibility to the effects of a drug due to its continued administration, resulting in the user's need to increase the dosage in order to achieve desired effects

withdrawal the physiological and psychological effects of discontinued use of a drug

PICTURE CREDITS

Index

Marc Kusinitz, Ph.D., is a science writer currently working freelance for *New Medical Science,* a bimonthly publication distributed to physicians. In addition to having served as news editor for the *New York State Journal of Medicine* and associate editor for *Scholastic Science World,* Dr. Kusinitz has written articles for *Science Digest* and *The New York Times.*

Solomon H. Snyder, M.D. is Distinguished Service Professor of Neuroscience, Pharmacology and Psychiatry at The Johns Hopkins University School of Medicine. He has served as president of the Society for Neuroscience and in 1978 received the Albert Lasker Award in Medical Research. He has authored *Uses of Marijuana, Madness and the Brain, The Troubled Mind, Biological Aspects of Mental Disorder,* and edited *Perspective in Neuropharmacology: A Tribute to Julius Axelrod.* Professor Snyder was a research associate with Dr. Axelrod at the National Institutes of Health.

Barry L. Jacobs, Ph.D., is currently a professor in the program of neuroscience at Princeton University. Professor Jacobs is author of *Serotonin Neurotransmission and Behavior* and *Hallucinogens: Neurochemical, Behavioral and Clinical Perspectives.* He has written many journal articles in the field of neuroscience and contributed numerous chapters to books on behavior and brain science. He has been a member of several panels of the National Institute of Mental Health.

Joann Ellison Rodgers, M.S. (Columbia), became Deputy Director of Public Affairs and Director of Media Relations for the Johns Hopkins Medical Institutions in Baltimore, Maryland, in 1984 after 18 years as an award-winning science journalist and widely read columnist for the Hearst newspapers.